1982

TWAYNE'S WORLD AUTHORS SERIES
A Survey of the World's Literature

SPAIN

Janet W. Diaz, Texas Tech University
EDITOR

Carmen Laforet

TWAS 601

Carmen Laforet

CARMEN LAFORET

By ROBERTA JOHNSON

Scripps College

TWAYNE PUBLISHERS

A DIVISION OF G. K. HALL & CO., BOSTON

Published in 1981 by Twayne Publishers,
A Division of G. K. Hall & Co.
All Rights Reserved

Printed on permanent/durable acid-free paper and bound
in the United States of America

First Printing

Library of Congress Cataloging in Publication Data

Johnson, Roberta, 1942–
Carmen Laforet

(Twayne's world authors series ; TWAS 601 : Spain)
Bibliography: pp. 147–50
Includes index.
1. Laforet, Carmen—Criticism and interpretation.
I. Title.
PQ6621.A38Z73   863'.62   80-22626
ISBN 0-8057-6443-7

To my mother

Contents

About the Author

Preface

Chronology

1. The Writer's Life   13
2. The Writer's Vocation   33
3. *Nada* (Nothing)   47
4. *La isla y los demonios* (The Island and the Devils),
   La mujer nueva (The New Woman), and *La insolación*
   (Sunstroke)   67
5. The Short Fiction   99
6. The Achievement   137
   Notes and References   143
   Selected Bibliography   147
   Index   151

About the Author

Roberta Johnson, Associate Professor of Spanish at Scripps College, holds B.A. and M.A. degrees from the University of California, Davis, and a Ph.D. from the University of California, Los Angeles. She has taught Spanish language and literature at Pomona College, Claremont Men's College, Wartburg College, Kansas State University, and Scripps College.

She has published articles on various twentieth century Spanish authors in *ES* (University of Valladolid), *Hispania*, *The Analysis of Hispanic Texts: Current Trends in Methodology*, *Los Ensayistas*, *Critical Essays on Gabriel Miró*, and *Letras Femeninas*. Professor Johnson is currently serving on the editorial boards of *Studies in Twentieth Century Literature* and *Letras Femeninas*, and she has been a Fulbright lecturer at the University of Valladolid, Spain, and a National Endowment for the Humanities Fellow in Residence at Duke University.

Preface

The purpose of this volume is to provide a general introduction to Carmen Laforet's life and works. Relatively little criticism exists on Laforet's work; there is only one book-length study (in Spanish) of this significant novelist of the post-Civil War period. Heretofore no book-length study in English has been available. Admittedly a book on a living writer can only be tentative, but my task in the present volume is somewhat eased in this respect by the long literary silence of Laforet. Her last piece of narrative fiction was published in 1963. I can therefore present a study of a body of her work (1944–1963) that will have a certain unity and definitive quality.

Sound critical analysis of Laforet's fiction has concentrated on the first novel *Nada* (Nothing). There are no in-depth articles on the other novels or the short fiction. I have taken into account this uneven critical situation, as well as probable reader familiarity with the works, in formulating my own approach to each segment of Laforet's fiction. In dealing with *Nada*, I have avoided a detailed plot summary (it is the novel most readers are likely to have read) and have briefly summed up the major critical interpretations. The bulk of the chapter on *Nada* is my own critical analysis of certain narrative features of the novel that have never been brought to light and which are important to Laforet's critical canon in general.

The other three novels receive more detailed plot summaries and are treated for the most part as comparisons and contrasts to the first novel. The purely literary analysis of these novels is more superficial, as their comparative literary merit and previous critical consideration would warrant. In presenting the short fiction, I have emphasized themes and narrative techniques that relate to the novels and to Laforet's growth and development as a narrator. I have taken care to outline amply the material contained in each story and novelette. I believe such an aid will be of interest to students, teachers, and scholars who wish to use this volume as a reference tool in searching for Spanish short fiction to fill a particular need: classroom reading, anthologies, or general studies.

In the life and times portion of the book, I have concentrated on the life, rather than on the times. Other volumes in this series give fine general analyses of the period in which Laforet grew up and began writing. Also, Laforet was not as involved as a child and adolescent in the major events of Spanish history in the 1920s and 1930s as were other writers of her generation. Since there is no other biography of Carmen Laforet, I have included many details of her life that are not available elsewhere. Her personal history is of immense interest in understanding her art and the trajectory of her literary production. The overriding consideration in preparing this volume was to study the artistic process of the individual writer—Carmen Laforet. To that end, I have used biography and journalism, but more than any other source, the testimony of the fictional works themselves.

I have employed a variety of critical methods in the analytical portions of the study, adapting my approach as each text seemed to require. In my analysis of *Nada*, for example, I combine exegetical close reading with concepts of narrative distance derived primarily from Wayne Booth's *The Rhetoric of Fiction*. In discussing the other novels and the stories, I rely more on the biographical, social, and historical framework in which they were written and which their action reflects. I have added a comprehensive section on the long novels, exploring the archetypal considerations these works suggest. While there are many constants in Carmen Laforet's work, each discrete piece contains something original—a theme or a means of focusing on a theme, a narrative technique—which I have made the center of my critical comments. Given the paucity of Laforet criticism and present limitations, the reader will understand that my statements are hardly exhaustive; for the most part I merely point in the direction that future analysis could take.

I would like to express my gratitude to Carmen Laforet, who generously met with me daily for a week in Rome in June 1976. Without her assistance, the biographical sections of this book would not have been possible. Thanks are also due my literature students at Wartburg College, who patiently listened to my analyses of several Laforet works, and to the Wartburg College Faculty Research and Publication Committee for several grants to carry out research for the book, including one to visit Laforet in Rome. And I wish to thank Professor Phillip A. Kildahl for his encouragement and Rita Little Ricaurte for her excellent assistance in typing the manuscript.

ROBERTA JOHNSON

Scripps College

Chronology

1921	Carmen Laforet born on September 6 in Barcelona.
1921–1939	Childhood and adolescence in Las Palmas, Gran Canaria.
1934	Mother dies and father remarries.
1939	Spanish Civil War ends. Laforet goes to Barcelona to live with grandparents and enrolls in the University of Barcelona as a humanities student.
1940–1942	Writes a few short stories and articles for Barcelona journals.
1942	Moves to Madrid and enrolls as a law student in the University of Madrid.
1944	Writes her first novel, *Nada* (Nothing), from January to September.
1945	Wins the first Nadal Prize for *Nada*, which is then published by *Destino*. Receives Fastenrath Prize.
1946	Marries Manuel Cerezales, editor, publisher, and journalist. First child, Marta, born.
1948	Birth of second child, Cristina.
1950	Third child, Silvia, born.
1951	Writes a regular column, "Puntos de vista de una mujer," for the journal *Destino*. Spiritual crisis and "conversion" to Catholicism.
1951–1958	Devotes much time to religious activities.
1952	Second novel, *La isla y los demonios* (The Island and the Devils), published. Fourth child, Manuel, born. *La muerta* (The Dead Woman), collection of short stories, published.
1954	Publishes *La llamada* (The Vocation), collection of novelettes.
1955	Publication of third novel, *La mujer nueva* (The New Woman).
1957	Birth of youngest child, Agustín.
1963	*La insolación* (Sunstroke), a novel, announced as first of a trilogy.
1965	Travels to the United States at the invitation of the State Department.

1967   Publishes *Paralelo 35* (Parallel 35), based on travel notes of the United States trip. Travels to Poland with lifelong friend Linka.

1970   Separates from Manuel Cerezales.

1971–
1972   Writes regular column for *ABC*, Madrid newspaper.

1975   Takes up residence in the Trastevere section of Rome.

CHAPTER 1

The Writer's Life

I Introduction

FOR many readers Carmen Laforet will always represent the eighteen-year-old adolescent searching for her own place in a world of tradition and change. This was the theme of *Nada* (Nothing), her first and to date best-known novel, which garnered her immediate fame when it received the first Nadal Prize in 1944. Her concerns in subsequent novels, *La isla y los demonios* (The Island and the Devils), *La mujer nueva* (The New Woman), *La insolación* (Sunstroke), and in many of her stories and short novels are similar. Even today, although she has published nothing but journal articles for over a decade, Laforet's life focuses on the progress of her children in their contemporary milieu; she is a person of great spirit who refuses to become sedentary or fossilized. When she does begin publishing again, her work will doubtless have the same freshness of insight into current contemporary life that it did in the 1940s and 1950s. But, even if Carmen Laforet should not venture into literary writing again, she would remain an important figure in post–Civil War Spanish literature for infusing new life into the bleak landscape of Spain's narrative fiction of the 1940s.

Before 1940 it is rare to find women in intellectual and artistic circles in Spain. Throughout the entire previous history of Spanish literature, the names of women writers can be counted on one hand: Santa Teresa, María Zayas de Sotomayor, Cecelia Böll de Faber, Emilia Pardo Bazán. In the twentieth century there have been few significant women writers in the literary generations before the Civil War (Generation of 1898, Generation of 1914, Generation of 1927), until in 1944 Carmen Laforet opened the doors through which a now impressive number of Spanish women writers have passed. Even today, however, women who manage to enter the

13

male-dominated bastions of Spanish letters have had an atypical life. Such is Carmen Laforet's case.

A knowledge of her biography is important, though not essential, to understanding her works. She herself claims that her novels and stories are not autobiographical, but it is not difficult to demonstrate that details of her life are fused with those of her characters to a greater degree than in the works of many novelists. Carmen Laforet, like Proust or Hemingway, whose lives are similarly related to their literary world, knows how to use autobiographical material to create a work of universal interest and significance. In later chapters on individual works, I will discuss how Laforet constructs the bridge between life and art.

The biographical information in this section comes primarily from conversations and correspondence I have had with the author herself; published biographical material on Carmen Laforet is scarce. I have not attempted the difficult and risky chore of culling biographical material from the literary works, although I have used her documentary book *Paralelo 35* and her travel and other journal articles for supplementary information. Writing biographies of living persons is difficult at best, and often the seeming advantage of firsthand information is more of a liability than an asset. An author may purposely or subconsciously distort interpretations of events that could be more objectively viewed from a greater distance, or the biographer may be burdened with so much knowledge and friendship that he does not see the forest for the trees. Suffice it to say that what I report here is a fraction of the story, limited primarily to information that is useful in understanding the fiction. A full biography will be in order at a much later date. Carmen Laforet is presently entering a new phase of her life, and there will doubtless be an entirely new chapter to add in five or ten years time.

II   *Carmen Laforet's Family; Childhood in the Canaries*

It is not surprising that the family in some form is the center of action in Laforet's four long novels and in much of the short fiction, since aspects of her own family history seem novelistic. Some of her more interesting ancestors, particularly on her father's side, contribute to the repertoire of stories she tells on social occasions. Her mother's family was very modest, with deep roots in Castile. Her maternal grandfather was a guard on an old Castilian estate in Toledo province, and the family was poor enough that her mother was eligible to attend a school for underprivileged girls administered by nuns. While her mother's side represents the stalwart peasantry of flat, stony, sparce Castile, her father's side is more romantically colorful, spiced with artists and soldiers. One branch was mostly Basque military people. Her paternal great-grandfather, Mariano Altolaguirre y Zumalacárregui, was a nephew of the generals Tomás Zumalacárregui, a Carlist (conservative and traditionalist), and Miguel Zumalacárregui (a liberal). Perhaps her attraction to the Cain and Abel theme in *Nada* (Nothing) can be traced to this conflicting political element in the family heritage.

The name Laforet is French from a French great-grandfather, who married a wealthy Sevillian woman. This great-grandmother is one of the more unusual individuals in Laforet's catalogue of ancestors, an example of the tradition of women with strength and character that is deeply rooted in both sides of the family. At fifty years of age, the great-grandmother married a man of thirty. They had one child, Laforet's grandfather, who was not allowed to marry until his mother died, although he and Laforet's grandmother were engaged for many years. The great-grandmother's husband never remarried. The paternal grandparents, with French ancestry on the grandfather's side and Basque lineage on the grandmother's side, upheld the family tradition of maintaining a residence in Seville.

Eduardo Laforet, the paternal grandfather, painted and taught drawing at the Balmes school in Barcelona. All seven of his children, including Laforet's father (who became an architect), could draw and paint. Laforet's own childhood was full of references to painters and sculptors, and on the walls of her childhood home hung many paintings. In fact, the most important item in the house was a painting by Murillo, one of the great Spanish masters, contemporaneous with El Greco and Velázquez, that her parents had inherited from the Sevillian branch of the family. The painting was a portrait of the Virgin the size of those in the Prado museum, but to Laforet it was much more beautiful than the Prado's Murillos, because it had never been restored. The painting had a cloudy film on it which young Carmen thought made it more poetic. It also had a scratch or burn in the area of the Virgin's entwined fingers, which Carmen's fertile childhood imagination transformed into an image of the Virgin smoking a Cuban cigar. She believes that she refrained from smoking until she was fairly mature because, even after she was old enough to see the true nature of the painting, the idea of cigar and cigarette smoke became confused in her subconscious with the smoke of the sacred incense burners: "Until I was twenty I did not smoke my first cigarette, and then I did it with a certain apprehension. But happily or unhappily, I'm not sure which, it did not taste like incense. I liked it."[1]

Art and architecture have always remained important to her. Once, while she was at the university, Laforet, who was not noted for her qualities as a student, shocked an art professor on her examination board with her insightful, sensitive answer to a question of art. After that demonstration, the professor invited her to attend all his art classes. Laforet's favorite painting is El Greco's *The Burial of Count Orgaz*, partly because it is a painting that cannot be reproduced. One must go to Toledo to the Santo Tomé church and see it there in its setting. Art and place are perhaps the two most consistently important elements in Laforet's fiction, and she achieves a fusion of them that marks a significant and unique contribution to the Spanish novel.

Carmen Laforet's mother and father met in Toledo, her mother's home town, where her mother was studying for a teaching degree and her father taught drawing and studied architecture. When her father finished his architectural degree, he took a teaching post in the Industrial School in Las Palmas on the island of Gran Canaria. Laforet lived her entire childhood and adolescence on the island (although she was actually born in Barcelona on September 6, 1921, during the summer recess). Her brothers, Eduardo and Juan, were born in the Canaries. That Laforet and her family were isolated from the political problems of mainland Spain during the 1920s and 1930s, particularly their remoteness from actual fighting during the Spanish Civil War (1936–1939), makes Carmen Laforet's formative years very different from those of her contemporaries Camilo José Cela, Miguel Delibes, Juan Goytisolo, Ana María Matute, and many others. When she did go to the mainland, immediately after the war, it was with fresh, curious eyes. She was able to capture the mood of Spain at that time as an insider (of Spanish heritage and language), but with an outsider's objectivity. This unique point of view is partly what gives *Nothing* its enduring qualities; it is not encumbered by the topicality of so many other Spanish works of this period.

Laforet's mother married her father when she was only eighteen, before she had an opportunity to practice her teaching career, but her training was not wasted. She was a natural teacher and brought up Laforet and her brothers reading the classics of Spanish literature. A few years before the mother's premature death (she died at thirty-three, when Carmen was only thirteen), she organized a session of reading aloud at the table after lunch. The mother would read a passage from *Don Quixote* or *Lazarillo de Tormes* and then would pass the book to one of the children for each to read several paragraphs; thus they read a chapter each day. Also at the children's request, their mother read many other books to them, among which were the works by the naturalist Fabre on the lives of birds and insects. Too, the Laforet children were allowed to select and read anything from the extensive family library that their level of ability could manage. During this period, Carmen was already demonstrating her own talent for narration, often entertaining her brothers with stories. But in order to disguise the fictional nature of what she told, she would introduce the imaginary tale by saying she had dreamt it.

At about the age of ten, Laforet began reading the *Episodios nacionales* (fictionalized versions of Spanish historical events) by her Canary Island compatriot Benito Pérez Galdós. What she found most attractive in the novels of Galdós was his ability to infuse his characters with life. The people in Galdós's books became so real for her and her brothers that they used their names in everyday conversations and made comparisons based on Galdosian character types: "Good as the priest Malvar" or "Stingy as doña Restituta Requejo."[2] One of the things Carmen Laforet herself strives for in her novels is the creation of characters who "live," but she does not achieve the same memorable characters that Galdós does, because her aesthetic principles and narrative techniques are very different. In searching for her literary parents (or grandparents) one is more likely to find them in Proust or Joyce than in Galdós. I do not suggest direct influence of either Proust or Joyce on the novel-writing of Carmen Laforet; it is not certain that she had read those authors by the time she wrote her first novel, at age twenty-two. But her artistic sensitivity has much more in common with the exploration of consciousness and the use of pictorial imagery germane to the European modernists than with the themes and techniques of her immediate Spanish literary ancestors.[3]

I leave a fuller discussion of Carmen Laforet's aesthetics and narrative techniques for later chapters in order to return to the subject at hand, Laforet's family background. The author was very fond of her mother, whom she describes as "a small woman with enormous spiritual energy, of sharp intelligence and an inflexible Castilian sense of duty."[4] She taught Laforet and her brothers the spiritual strength in truth, not to leave things half done, and to accept the consequences of their actions. She was a kind person who had the gift of friendship; many people still remember her vividly in Las Palmas. Friendship is of the greatest importance in Laforet's own life and is a recurrent leitmotif in her works. She comments upon this aspect of life, about which she learned first from her mother:

The novelist D. H. Lawrence in a letter to Huxley, if I remember correctly, says that he believes that there exists a sworn friendship which is more profound, stronger and more indestructible than love and marriage—a friendship that exists between a man and another man or between two women or between a man and a woman, but, he added, "I have never found such a friendship, although I know it exists." I can attest without fear of being mistaken at this point in my life that I *have* found such a friendship, and that it has been given me, not once, but, to my good fortune, several times in my life.[5]

In discussing Laforet's student years, I will detail several friendships that have had continuing influence in her life and that are recreated in her books.

Laforet's father had many talents and interests, aside from the plastic arts by which he made his living. He played the piano well and was an avid sportsman who encouraged his children to pursue these interests. He was anxious that Carmen learn to play the piano, but she had little talent for music. Rather than practice seriously, she would mechanically do her scales while reading a book of stories she placed on the music stand. Her mother discovered the subterfuge one day and decided that Carmen should discontinue the piano lessons. Laforet's father did not distinguish between his male and female children when it came to encouraging their participation in outdoor activities. They swam, sailed, hiked, and cycled. Her father, who had been a competitive cyclist in his youth, had once been champion at pistol-shooting in Spain. He collected firearms and kept a shooting range on the grounds of their home in Monte Coello. These interests were perhaps attributable to the military branch of the family. Carmen entered into most of the sporting activities her father encouraged, but she resisted when he invited her to partic- ipate in home shooting matches. The father could not understand that his daughter abhorred firearms and tried to convince her that there was nothing more feminine than carrying a tiny pistol in one's purse. She was never able to achieve "femininity" by this means. The sporting side of life figures very little in Laforet's novels, whereas artists and artistic elements (also derived from her father's interests) prevail over all other concerns. Perhaps one scene in *Nothing* can be associated with a negative reaction on Laforet's part to her father's love of firearms. Andrea overreacts to seeing Román handling a pistol in front of her friend Ena, thereby causing the dramatic episode that serves as a kind of climax to the novel.

After her mother's death, Laforet's father remarried, but neither Carmen nor her brothers liked their stepmother. She says of the father's second wife that "in spite of my great resistance to believing in fairy tales, she reaffirmed their truth, acting like the stepmothers in those stories. From her I learned that fantasy always falls short compared to reality (and that before having read Dostoyevsky!)."[6] Mothers and their surrogates play an important role in Carmen Laforet's fiction; in the conclusion to the chapters on Laforet's novels I will discuss the significance of the mother figure and her substi- tutes in the characters' lives and for the meaning of the novels. The unpleasant family situation after her father's remarriage had its pos- itive side in Laforet's life, however, for she enjoyed much more freedom of movement than most Spanish girls her age. After classes she was free to go for a swim at the beach if she wished, because she did not have to return home for the midday meal, normally a sacred family institution in Spain. One can swim all year round in the Canaries, and Laforet particularly enjoyed the beach in winter when there were no tourists.

Thus she led a somewhat picaresque existence during her last five years in the Islands, developing a love of freedom that continues to manifest itself in her life and in her books. She often skipped classes during those years; she always missed Physics, and since Literature followed immediately after Physics, she skipped that, too, sending her compositions to class with a friend. When the Literature teacher asked Laforet's friends where she was, they replied that she was ill, but one day the teacher saw her in the street and confronted her. The instructor said that even if she could write better than Cervantes (her writing talent was already becoming evident), she would not pass the course without attending class. The next day, true to her picaresque fashion, she attended school all day, but rather than going to all the classes in which she was enrolled, she devoted the entire day to attending all the classes of the Literature teacher.

Laforet had many friends in the Canaries, and she still maintains correspondence with some of them. During the Civil War she developed a friendship with a young Literature professor from Madrid, Consuelo Burell. Professor Burell described for Laforet the intellectual ferment in the university before the war and the importance of the Institución Libre de Enseñanza for Spanish culture. She also told Carmen anecdotes about writers and eminent professors, who were friends or parents of friends. Carmen became enthusiastic about the lives of these people and wanted to know them. She did meet some of them later when she went to Madrid in the 1940s, but, unfortunately, many were already exiled.

Carmen Laforet's parents were apolitical, and the Civil War (1936–1939) was not a significant issue in her family. The Canary Islands saw no bombings or other direct involvement in the conflict; the Islanders received news of the mainland battles and that was all. However, given that the Canaries were one of Franco's strongholds, the sentiments of the people were generally pro-Nationalist, and Carmen herself hoped that all those poor people (in the Republican zone) would soon be "freed" from the horrors she read about in the papers and heard of on the radio. As soon as hostilities ended in 1939, eighteen-year-old Carmen went to Barcelona to study Humanities at the university. Although she has only returned to the Islands once since she left, her formative years there shape her artistic vision, not only because of the historical isolation of the Canaries, but for the sense of space they gave her. The year-round garden spot, which the Canaries are, surely contributed to Laforet's sensual approach to memory and space. She often combines sight, smell, and other senses to evoke a remembered place or time. She says of her father, for example, that "he was accustomed to smoking a pipe and used an excellent English tobacco mixture whose odor has remained with me—as has that of those enclosed corridors of the house in Las Palmas—as one of those unmistakable smells of my childhood."[7]

III   *The University of Barcelona*

When Carmen Laforet arrived in Barcelona in 1939, she found a hungry, devastated city, the ambience described in *Nothing*. But hunger—and Laforet, like most Spaniards, was often hungry in those days—could not take away her enthusiasm for new experiences, her curiosity, and her desire to participate in the life of this entirely new place. In Barcelona Laforet met interesting friends, through whom she discovered whole new worlds. She met many Catalan young people, who had been evacuated to France near the end of the Civil War and who had had to return to Spain because of the Second World War, after beginning their university studies in Montpellier. Two friendships are of key importance during her Barcelona period in the early 1940s. One of them was with Concha Ferrer, the leader of Laforet's group, with whom she still maintains a strong relationship some thirty years later. When Laforet met her, Concha was having to repeat her high-school work, even though she had already gone to the university in France. At that time (under the Franco regime) her Catalan diploma was not valid. Until a few years before his death in 1975, Franco's policy was to suppress the other languages of the Peninsula in an effort to eliminate all traces of regional culture, autonomy, and pride.

Concha studied with a sporting spirit and a will of iron. She worked in the mornings, and then she and Carmen would get together with friends at the Ateneo (gathering place of the literary circle). Once a week Concha invited the group to her residence to share the luxuries of a package from her family. Her family surmounted all kinds of difficulties to send her this package, which contained canned goods, cheese, sweets, and a huge loaf of white bread—a rare item in those days. Concha's family feared, and with reason, that she was not getting proper nourishment in Barcelona. Together they consumed the contents of the package in ten minutes, lacing it with a *porrón* of wine (a *porrón* is a glass *bota*, typically found in working-class bars in Spain, which allows each member of the group to drink from the same vessel without touching his lips to it). The principal topic of conversation at those gatherings was life in Catalonia before the war, and they generally spoke in Catalan. Although Laforet understands Catalan, she has never learned to speak it. In fact, she has always resisted learning foreign languages even though she has traveled extensively throughout Europe and the United States. Her lively character sustains her in most situations, and the many misunderstandings she has, because she does not know languages, simply add to the repertoire of stories she is so fond of telling.

Linka is the second friendship from Laforet's Barcelona years that she maintains to this day. Linka's family, which is Polish, came to Spain in 1939 seeking refuge from the German and Russian invasions into Poland. They immediately became Laforet's second family by mutual adoption. Carmen lived with her grandparents in Barcelona and was virtually a prisoner in their home, so that going to Linka's house on Montcada Street (a house that belonged to a Catalan branch of Linka's family) was an escape. Montcada Street was in centuries past the location of many noblemen's city homes; some of these spacious palaces, with their courtyards, where the horse-drawn carriages entered to pick up their distinguished owners, are still standing. The street even in the 1940s was beginning to have a reputation as a center for artists, and today several of the fine and partially restored old palaces house the Picasso Museum and some of Barcelona's finest privately owned commercial art galleries. The area is close to several of Barcelona's other more interesting districts: the Gothic quarter and Cathedral, the harbor area, with its famous little church, Santa María del Mar, and the infamous *barrio chino* (red-light district). One can easily imagine the impact these varied sights and experiences had on a very curious Carmen Laforet, who had lived nearly all her life until age eighteen in the remote Canary Islands. *Nothing* recalls in vivid spatial descriptions the atmosphere of these sections of Barcelona.

Through Linka's family, which was constantly seeking news of the events in Europe and the progress of the Second World War, Laforet broadened her interests beyond the narrow limits of Spain. Linka and Carmen continually asserted their faith in an Allied victory. (The official Spanish position was neutrality, but it was no secret that Franco favored the Axis Powers, which had helped him during the Civil War.) Linka and Carmen fantasized about the end of the war when the borders would open up, the bakeries would miraculously fill with bread, and the bookstores would stock fabulously interesting books. Although life was militarized and dangerous, Laforet relished the element of adventure. Linka's family was involved in Polish refugee operations in Barcelona, and Laforet's adventuresome spirit led her to assist them, mainly in escorting illegal aliens from the *barrio chino* to other parts of the city. Her friend Linka was even jailed for a time for these activities. Laforet's parents, her father in particular, had never made her feel that some activities were reserved for men only; she grew up with a sense that she could do anything that desire and opportunity might present. Part of what Laforet wanted to achieve in writing *Nothing* was to recapture the atmosphere of post–Civil War Barcelona, but she deliberately left out references to the European war because it would have been artistically diffuse and thus confusing.

Barcelona offered many new worlds to Laforet and she did not hesitate to enter any of them. She became involved with a group of artists that met every afternoon in the Virreina Palace, a center of artistic recuperation after the war. Laforet was the only girl to frequent the gathering regularly, although Linka sometimes accompanied her. Carmen loved to roam the streets of the city (she still does), and in her wanderings she met a wide variety of people. One time she invited a little old lady to have coffee and *churros* (stick-shaped donuts) with her—a special treat for which she seldom had the money. The lady told her her life story. Another time she encountered a young portrait painter who wanted to paint her likeness. Although he was an excellent painter, he finally abandoned the attempt to paint Carmen because he could not reproduce her expression. Laforet has an extraordinary face, not beautiful, but with a liveliness that would be hard to capture on canvas. Her most distinguished features are piercing, dark, almond-shaped eyes and striking high cheekbones.

Laforet associated with other students at the university as well. (All Spanish students have a *pandilla*, a group with whom they gather every day in the cafés or the patios of the university or with whom they take long strolls through the streets to talk about their studies and other interests.) Once when Carmen went to the beach with her university friends, she was fined by the police for wearing a swimsuit that did not have a skirt on it and for sunning herself in a bathing suit without putting on her terry-cloth beach coat. Her life in the carefree Canaries had not prepared her for the more puritanical mainland.

IV *Madrid: The First Novel*

In September of 1942 Laforet moved to Madrid, where she established contact with her mother's family and entered into their

world of recent memories of the Civil War. And she continued her
intimate association with Linka's family, since they too had recently
moved to Madrid. Laforet enrolled in the law school at the University of Madrid and studied at the Ateneo in the afternoon, often
staying there until it closed. Then she would wander about the
silent city streets (there were few cars in the capital in those days).
She never hurried home to her house at the end of Pardinas Street,
preferring solitude under the transparent, starry Madrid sky.

Carmen and Linka took numerous trips around the Castilian countryside, sometimes alone and sometimes with Linka's fiancé, Pablo.
They would board the always overcrowded trains and go out to
neighboring villages and cities. Fuel, as well as food, was scarce
after the Civil War, a situation intensified by the European war.
The aisleways and the compartments of the trains were overflowing
with people, suitcases, bags of food, and live chickens that sometimes escaped cackling from the straw bags in which they were
carried. On occasion the train cars were so full that the travelers
had to descend through a window at their station. The trains were
exceedingly slow, and the passengers arrived at their destinations
covered in coal dust. The trip from Madrid to Ávila took at least
five hours, if there were no delays (there almost always were). That
trip takes an hour today. In spring or summer, upon reaching Ávila
or whatever their destination, Laforet and her companions would
swim in the river, be it the Tagus or the Adaja, to wash off the layer
of coal dust. All these inconveniences seemed a small price to pay
for the joy of exploring the old Castilian cities and surrounding
countryside.

While engaged in these activities—studies and excursions—Carmen Laforet wrote her first novel, between January and September
of 1944, at the age of twenty-two. Actually Laforet had begun her
literary career during her three years in Barcelona by writing some
short stories, published in local journals. Unfortunately most of
these youthful efforts have been lost. Her very first publications
were vignettes sent to the magazine *Mujer*. The journal normally
did not accept unsolicited collaborations, but the editor printed
Laforet's pieces because they were good. He wrote her a letter
saying that he had almost not answered her, since she had not
included return postage. *Nothing*, a product of the young adult
Carmen Laforet, thus stands as the first extant record of a talent for
narration that had begun to emerge in early childhood. When La-

foret finished the manuscript of *Nothing*, she did not know what to do with it or of whom to inquire as to whether it might be published. Linka directed Laforet to her friend Manuel Cerezales, a sometime journalist and literary critic, who was involved at the time in a small publishing company specializing in history books. Cerezales liked the novel and suggested that she submit it to Editorial Destino in Barcelona, which had just announced a competition for a novel prize in their magazine, the Nadal Prize, to be conferred for the first time in 1945. She sent the novel to the contest, not so much for the prize, which she believed she had little chance of winning, but hoping at least to interest Destino in publishing the novel. To her great surprise, she was awarded the 5,000-peseta Nadal Prize, and the novel became an immediate and long-lasting success. That same year the Fastenrath Prize of the Real Academia Española was also bestowed on *Nothing*, further attesting to the novel's impact on the Spanish literary establishment.

Rafael Vázquez Zamora, who was on the Nadal Prize selection committee, recalls:

My colleagues were in Barcelona, while I was in Madrid. About Christmas-time when there was a great deal of snow, I remember that I was carrying everywhere, even at the risk of losing them, the loose sheets of the original manuscript (rather badly typed and without correction) of a novel entitled *Nothing*, which had impressed me from the first moment. A girl arrived in a large Catalan city from the country, and was entering a world of nightmares. The young girl, named Andrea, was going to live with relatives: her grandmother, her uncles and aunts—whom she had not known until then—because she was going to study in Barcelona. The novel had a tremendous "impact" and stood out signally among the others presented by the contestants, thrust forward by its quality. It was undoubtedly an innovation in what was being written in Spain. Besides, it had the unmistakable flavor, or authenticity, of something experienced and transformed into literature. Moreover, I was quite surprised that it had been written by a woman.[8]

The older, established writers of Spain took note of the sudden appearance of this promising young woman writer. Azorín (one of the few remaining members of the by then hallowed Generation of 1898), Juan Ramón Jiménez, and Francisco·Ayala wrote public letters about the event, and Ramón Sender wrote Laforet a private letter from his exile in the New World. Azorín wrote in *Destino*, indirectly praising Laforet's fresh new kind of novel-writing:

Carmen, you have done something that is unworthy of you, in my opinion;
I have been vacillating for a long time now, days, weeks; I could not bring
myself to blame or reproach, to accuse you as I am going to do in *continenti*.
I am going to do it because my conscience requires that I do it. And so
what is this that you have done? What is it that provokes my indignation?
It is *Nothing*, a beautiful book! And if you should take up the pen, heaven
forbid, to write another novel, let it not be like *Nothing*; I mean, not a
new novel, but rather a run-of-the-mill, pedestrian, long-winded novel
without detailed and careful observations, without psychological insights
that make us think and feel.[9]

Juan Ramón Jiménez, seemingly incapable of understanding the
new novelistic mode that Carmen Laforet had introduced, was less
generous:

It does not seem to me that your book is a novel in the usual sense of the
word, because of the plot, or even in the more specialized sense of the
word as in the case of the aesthetic novel, but it is a series of very beautiful
stories, some of them, like those of Gorki, Eça de Queiroz, Unamuno or
Hemingway. And I believe this so firmly that in my view *Nothing* falters
in Chapter Nineteen, that is to say, when a coherent novelistic plot is
declared.[10]

Laforet was astonished by the interest her literary success fostered
in her as a person, and she was amazed at the interviews and
questions that ensued. She felt she would be unable to continue
writing until the hullabaloo subsided, and people stopped asking
her, "What are you writing now?"

V *Marriage; Children; More Novels and Stories*

In 1946 the student phase of Laforet's life, filled with carefree
university days, wandering city streets at night, and weekend excursions, ended. The next phase, her marriage to Manuel Cerezales
and her life as a wife and mother, lasted for twenty-four years until
1970, when she and Cerezales separated. Laforet's five children
were born between 1946 and 1957—first the three girls: Marta
(November 1946), Cristina (April 1948), Silvia (April 1950); and then
the two boys: Manuel (October 1952) and Agustín (May 1957). The
exigencies of raising a family and certain restraints on married
women in Spain made writing more difficult for her in her new

roles. During the first three years after the publication of *Nothing*, Laforet did not write at all; then she wrote some short stories and numerous newspaper and journal articles on personal, human interest, and travel topics between 1947 and 1963. It was seven years before the second novel appeared; *La isla y los demonios* (The Island and the Devils) was published in February of 1952, when she was pregnant with her fourth child. The public that had received *Nothing* with such acclaim was beginning to dismiss her as a novelist with only one novel to write. *The Island* was welcomed as a fine second effort, which, though not as fresh and startling as the first novel, indicated certain technical refinements and gave hope that a promising writer was continuing to develop her skills.

The stories Laforet published in journals in the seven years between *Nothing* and *The Island and the Devils* were collected in the volume *La muerta* (The Dead Woman) in 1952. These stories fall into categories corresponding to several phases of her life between 1941 and 1951. Perhaps the earliest is "Última noche" (The Last Night), which Laforet would prefer not to have included in her complete works. It was written during her years at the University of Barcelona (before *Nothing*), for a friend who was looking for short stories about World War II for a collection. He needed one by a French writer, and Laforet suggested that she furnish one since a story with a French setting, signed by C. Laforet, could easily seem French. Laforet's spirit of adventure and sense of humor, as well as her lack of reverence for academic categories, are evident in this incident.

Nearly all Spanish novelists participate actively in journalism. In 1951 Laforet regularly wrote a column entitled "Puntos de vista de una mujer" (From a Woman's Point of View) for *Destino*, a weekly magazine published in Barcelona. In 1971 her "Diario de Carmen Laforet" (Diary of Carmen Laforet) appeared several times a week in *ABC*, Madrid's leading newspaper, and she has contributed many other articles to a wide variety of newspapers and magazines. Laforet's journalistic writing has almost always appeared during periods of her life when she has reached a temporary impasse on a novel in progress or when she has temporarily put more strictly literary writing aside. Thus journalism is an important source of continuing vitality to her writing career. Only recently has any of Laforet's journalism been collected,[11] but, unfortunately, a comprehensive collection is nearly impossible, because Laforet has not kept copies of all her work, or even a list of all her journal contributions. This aspect of her writing has never received any critical attention, and much of it (produced in great haste under the pressure of deadlines) does not warrant extensive scrutiny. However, some of the articles have literary merit and reveal aspects of Laforet's personality and art that are helpful in appreciating her literary works.

Even though Carmen Laforet's life took a very different path after her marriage, and the new responsibilities limited the things she loved most—travel, adventure, new scenery, and friends—her life continued to be a search; in her words, "it becomes an interior adventure."[12] In 1951 she underwent a spiritual crisis in which, after a quasi-mystical experience that occurred on a Madrid street one day, she "converted" to Catholicism. Although she, like most Spaniards, had been nominally brought up in the Catholic faith, her family was not particularly religious, and Laforet did not really practice her religion either as a child or as a young adult. Because of the strong emphasis on the Church as an institution under the Franco regime and the rigidity with which the dogma was presented at that time, Laforet found it difficult to carry out her newly discovered faith. The spirit of dogmatism is basically contrary to her freedom-loving, searching, questioning nature. She struggled with her new religious faith, attempting to reconcile some of her misgivings about dogma for nearly seven years, until she finally decided that she, like Don Quixote, was tilting against windmills. She concluded that it was not essential to understand religion in the rational way toward which she had been striving.

Laforet wrote *La mujer nueva* (The New Woman), published in 1955, at the encouragement of her husband, to reveal in literature the mystic experience she had undergone. Although the novel was awarded the Premio Menorca, it received relatively little press at the time of its publication and has had almost no critical attention. The few articles that have been written on it are authored by churchmen, concerned solely with its theological value. To the wider public interested in the career of the young woman who had written *Nothing*, one of whose virtues is its nonpartisan view, *The New Woman* signaled a Carmen Laforet who had gone parochial. The incessant questions about her own conversion inspired by the publication of *The New Woman* so exhausted and traumatized Laforet that she was unable to write for a time. While working on *The New*

Woman, Laforet was also writing a series of novelettes, published in 1954 (one year before *The New Woman*) with the title *La llamada* (The Vocation). Several of the novelettes, especially "The Vocation" and "El último verano" (The Last Summer), disclose a spirit of Christian charity surely related to her conversion and work in the Church at this time. Other novelettes written about this period, but not included in the collection, as well as several isolated short stories, reflect the same concerns.

The exhaustion produced by writing and responding to the attention given *The New Woman* lifted after a period of rest, interspersed with several trips abroad in the late 1950s, and Laforet began to plan a trilogy, *Tres pasos fuera del tiempo* (Three Steps Out of Time). She published the first volume, *La insolación* (Sunstroke), in 1963, but by the time she received the galley proofs for the second volume, *Jaque mate* (Checkmate), several years later, her concept of the trilogy had changed significantly. A period of family crisis prevented her from making the extensive revisions she now felt necessary before the work could be published. The projected new title for the revised second volume is *Jaque y cuento* (Check and Tale). Laforet believes that because Western society has undergone such radical changes since the 1940s (the temporal setting of the first volume), the remaining novels could better portray the differing generations. As she was thinking through the revisions necessary to make the second volume conform to her revised concept of the trilogy, she spent a great deal of time in the periodicals libraries in Madrid, researching newspapers to recapture the ambience of the postwar years. She encountered all kinds of bizarre articles in the Spanish journals of the 1940s and 1950s (like the notice of a cat born with wings), mostly designed to keep the attention of the Spanish people from the penury of their existence. In the 1960s Laforet could read with an ironic perspective the Spanish reports in the 1940s of food shortages and starving people in Europe. The official Spanish press, trying to minimize the severe hunger the Spaniards were suffering after the Civil War, published exaggerated accounts of the deprivation caused in the rest of Europe by the Second World War. Few Spaniards traveled to Europe at that time, but those who did, Laforet recalls, car ied large amounts of food with them, believing, from the Spanish newspaper reports, that there was nothing at all to eat in Europe.

Laforet made two extensive and personally important trips in

1965 and 1967. The first was to the United States at the invitation
of the State Department, after which she published her travel notes
as *Paralelo 35*, a title imposed on her by the editor. In the book
she projects her still-youthful enthusiasm over the most banal-seem-
ing incidents: a visit to a Sara Lee factory for frozen pastries or the
sound of an American housewife vacuuming the carpets before the
rest of the family and the guests arise in the morning (Spanish
housewives of Carmen Laforet's economic status would have servants to do housework). A highlight of the American trip was meeting Ramón Sender in California. Sender had left Spain after the
war, but he read *Nothing* when it was published and wrote Laforet
a warm, congratulatory letter. The two Spanish novelists embraced
in the California sunshine, something they would not be able to do
for many years in Spain. Laforet attended the banquet given for
Sender at the Ateneo in Madrid in 1974, celebrating his return to
Spain for the first time in thirty-five years.

In 1967 she made a trip to Poland, sponsored by the journal
Actualidad, for which she did a series of articles on that country.
Linka accompanied her, and many of her most memorable experiences were with Linka's family, a stalwart lot, that had bravely
resisted the onslaught of Russians and Germans alike. Laforet and
Linka relived some of the spirit of adventure they had shared in
Barcelona in the 1940s, going by train from Madrid to Paris, where
they planned to spend two weeks, believing it would take that long
to get visas from the Polish consulate, where, true to postwar Polish
style, there are endless lines for everything. The day they arrived
in Paris, the Polish consulate was closed because the consul was
giving a party. They spoke to a man at the door, who took their
documents upstairs to the consul. Surprisingly, they received their
visas immediately; had the consulate been open, the whole process
would have taken weeks. The incident reveals some of the
lighthearted ironies of life that have helped Laforet keep her sense
of humor and proportion through even the most oppressive times.

This first adventure at the Polish consulate set the tone for a trip
replete with amusing situations that began restoring some of Laforet's spirit of adventure, a spirit she had been losing during twenty
years of married life and the responsibilities of motherhood. The
two nearly middle-aged ladies, acting like twenty-year-olds, took
a train for Warsaw that very day on a first-class coach. After the
train was underway, they discovered that there would be no food

served in the car until the following morning. They had failed to eat in the excitement of obtaining visas and making travel arrangements. The train was extremely slow, and first-class passengers, locked inside their cars, were not allowed to descend at the stations. At midnight they were awakened by the smell of sausage being sold at a station by an ambulatory vendor, and they shouted, amidst giggles and titters, for the sausage to be brought to their window.

Intuition and spontaneity are the keys to Carmen Laforet's personality and life. Another example of these salient aspects of her personality is her handling of the quantities of mail she has received since the success of *Nothing* and her subsequent literary career. For a time she had a secretary, who opened her letters and answered many of them. But when she is in charge of her own correspondence, she often leaves many letters unopened. She decides which letters to read by the impression she receives from the handwriting.

VI *The Present and Future*

The trips away from home and Spain and the maturation of her children helped Laforet to initiate the third phase of her life, which began with her marital separation in 1970. Laforet is currently in a state of transition from her previous life as a mother and housewife to her probable future as a once-more productive writer. The most important experience of this phase to date has been her taking up residence in the Trastevere section of Rome, where she is rediscovering the rewards of meeting new and unexpected friends, just as she did some thirty years ago on the streets of Barcelona. She has met and become friends with Rafael Alberti, a well-known exiled Spanish poet, and María Teresa León, who live near her in the Trastevere. Perhaps her most important encounter has been with Pablo Lafuente, the exiled novelist and friend of Alberti, whom she met on his deathbed in Rome. Laforet was impressed by his intelligence, sense of humor, and strength of spirit, even at the moment when his life was about to end. At seventy, the dying Lafuente was still a young man, still very much concerned that his great dream of having his novels published in Spain be fulfilled. Laforet attended Lafuente's funeral, along with a large group of people of all nationalities. This encounter with a dying writer, who had left his last novel unfinished and who continued to think of his work, even as death approached, gave Laforet the courage to begin a book on the people she has met during her residence in the Trastevere. The book should be near completion. I will abstain from the temptation to speculate about what we can expect from Carmen Laforet after the book of encounters in the Trastevere. There will doubtless be more fiction, because Laforet is a natural storyteller, and she has many more stories to write.

CHAPTER 2

The Writer's Vocation

I Introduction

CARMEN Laforet writes as she lives—in a spontaneous fashion: "I know that my books come from a deep love of life," she says.[1] But while she recognizes that her vocation for writing is innate, she is not a disciplined writer, producing a certain number of pages every day, whether in the mood or not. She acknowledges her strengths and limitations as a professional writer in the "Introduction" to the first (and only) volume of her complete works:

If God allows me to live, I believe that in a few years there will be a second volume of my complete works. If I believe this, it is not because I have great confidence in my capacity for hard work—I am not a cheerful worker —, I have acquired through difficult experience in my life the faith that if one is a writer, one always writes, even though one does not want to, even though one tries to escape this dubious glory and this genuine suffering that goes with the vocation.[2]

In this chapter I let Carmen Laforet speak for herself, through her journal articles and introductions to her books, as to how she works and what is aesthetically important to her. It was made clear in the previous chapter that she spends long periods of time without writing, but her experiences during these nonproductive times are informing new articles, stories, and novels that will emerge in writing later on:

Summer has ended. It has ended for me at least because I find a disconcerting sheaf of empty sheets of paper on my desk, all of which I should have been filling during these past months and which have remained waiting for the fresh air and soft light of the end of September to oblige me to return to them. . . . Eight days each year one can hear a short course on Saint John of the Cross or on Saint Teresa, treated with extraordinary

33

authority and seriousness. It is truly a summer spiritual exercise, a spiritual exercise drunk from the jug of the Saints, who are at the same time two writers of unending interest. All Ávila, with the freshness of her stones and the fervor of her Saints has worked for me in these eight days of my summer. I have seen from inside, illuminated by the sober and extremely authoritative word of Baldomero Jiménez, rector of the Ávila Seminary, the mystic work of the Saint and I have traversed with her the route of her foundations, this route strewn with small, happy, white Carmelite houses, houses of prayer, mortification and joy, which after so many centuries continue to open up all over the world, carrying an aroma of Spanish spirituality from almost polar regions to the tropics.[3]

Because the principal source of Laforet's literary raw materials is her lived experience, she has been working—gathering material and spiritual energy—even though she has not written a word.

Her other stockpile of subjects is rooted in anecdotes about her family and items of curiosity read and collected over the years. Like any good raconteur, she has an inexhaustible supply of stories at hand and can recall and adorn them when the appropriate occasion arises:

I want to write some stories as gifts for my children, stories about people that existed and whose names I know, the thread of an anecdote I heard narrated, without paying much attention, when I was a girl. They are characters that form links in a chain broken in many places. They are great grandparents, great great grandparents, ancestors unknown to me. I enjoy inventing things about them that I know and even more what I do not know about their histories. But here I am without writing, gathering books around me, arranging pens upon the table and on top of old projects, looking for pretexts not to get to work.[4]

Clearly the material is there, as well as the writer's vocation, but when confronted with the choice between writing about life and experiencing it directly, Carmen Laforet prefers the latter. This preference has surely been a serious obstacle to her publishing.

II *Formative Influences*

Carmen Laforet's literary style is unselfconscious and unschooled. Although she has read widely (if unsystematically), and especially admires Galdós, Salinas, members of the Generation of 1898, the

Russian novelists, and Proust, she has no specific master. Neither her technique, themes, nor any other aspect of her art can be readily traced to a specific model or source.[5] Her talent for narration is natural, as are her insights into life, people, and situations. She works primarily on intuition. These characteristics, coupled with an avoidance of intellectualizing, give her novels and stories a ring of authenticity. Laforet does very little correcting of manuscripts. She sends them to the publisher just as they come from the type-writer the first time through:

I understand that I do not have the long patience of a genius. At least, in terms of style it is impossible for me to correct a book. If some of my pages sound like correct and harmonious Castilian, it is because it came out of my pen that way, spontaneously. . . . What I, as a novelist, am concerned about in my books, what I am perfectly capable of entirely destroying and redoing as many times as necessary, is their structure and also their life. I try to avoid writing essays; I shun explaining my own cultural opinions, which I consider of very little interest, and give that for which I think I have talent: Observation, the creation of life. I am careful to state these events objectively so that the reader can judge them for himself, become interested in them, and accept them or reject them as he sees fit.[6]

Laforet says she is not interested in attempting to incorporate into her writing style the innovative narrative techniques initiated by James Joyce and William Faulkner (e.g., stream of consciousness, run-on sentences, and extreme achronology) or in the developments of the French *nouveau roman*. However, the elliptical nature of the narrative in *Nothing* is revolutionary enough in the Spanish fiction of its time to suggest some contagion from the new novelistic prac-tices of Europe. I suggest in Chapter 4 the possible influences of Faulkner on *La isla y los demonios* (The Island and the Devils), particularly in the revolving viewpoint of the death scene. Laforet is unfamiliar with the latest generation of Spanish novelists, in-cluding Juan Benet and Luis Goytisolo, who self-consciously cul-tivate Faulknerian techniques, but she is well acquainted with the members of her own generation: Miguel Delibes, Camilo José Cela, and Ana María Matute.

Like Delibes, Laforet began her literary career with the narrative, and it is the only genre she has ever attempted (many Spanish novelists, including Camilo José Cela, began by writing poetry). Laforet shares with the early Delibes an aversion to extreme in-

novation in narrative technique, preferring a straightforward, fairly
chronological style. But Delibes has now broken that preference in
such works as the autodialogued *Cinco horas con Mario*, the alle-
gorical *Parábola del náufrago*, and the second-person narration of
Las guerras de nuestros antepasados, while Laforet's narrative techniques have not evolved appreciably. However, she stopped writing
fiction in 1963 about the time Delibes and other Spanish novelists
were discovering new approaches to narrative. The form her future
books will take is impossible to guess, but her aesthetic position has
not yet changed significantly. She is still more concerned with theme
and ambience than with revolutionary narrative technique; narration comes naturally to her without con cious effort. Even so, some
of her short fiction, especially the novelettes, seems to be a narrative
experiment exploring alternative means of handling certain characters and problems.

III   *Creation of Space*

As Laforet herself has understood, the strongest elements in her
novels and stories are her characters and her ability to recreate
situations, particularly a sense of place. She loves places and has
an extraordinary spatial memory. For example, she once went on
an excursion to Toledo with a group of fellow law students from the
University of Madrid. She was enchanted by the city and still recalls
the details and ecstasy of the day (her memory is of Toledo before
tourism became the single most important enterprise in Spain, and
the city—a favorite with foreigners—filled with trinket shops and
tour buses). All Laforet's friends remember what fun she was on
that day, assuming that their company made her so jubilant, when
actually her enthusiasm was generated by the city. She scarcely
noticed her companions at all. Laforet has returned to Toledo many
times. On one visit with her younger son, Agustín, she happened
onto a church with the tomb of Garcilaso de la Vega (a great poet
of the Spanish Renaissance) alongside that of his father. She was so
astonished to see that the sculptor had made the two icons exactly
alike that she wrote an article about it.

Her talent for vivid recreation of scene is so great that, before
her trip to Poland with Linka, her friend suggested they go somewhere together; Linka reminded her that they had only taken one
trip together—to the Canaries. Laforet was surprised at this remark

because she and Linka had never gone to the Canaries together. In fact, she has only returned to the Islands once since leaving as a young girl. Linka was thinking of a story Laforet had written about such a trip during their Barcelona years. The impression of being in the Canaries was so strong that Linka actually remembered having gone there with her friend. The story has unfortunately been lost, along with so many other pieces Laforet has written at various periods in her life. She does not destroy her writing as some fastidious writers do, but she loses things because of her lack of organization and her unconcern for matters that pertain to the past and the future. Hers is a life that centers on the present moment.

Though the story set in the Canaries has been lost, a travel article on the Islands that Laforet wrote for *ABC* during her visit there in 1951 gives an idea of the author's attachment to the place:

This South does not have the sensuality [of the North]; it has passion; it is charred, devastated in its warm, deep silence, and tremendous, crepuscular skies; the colors of blood and violets envelop it in the afternoon. At midday, the rocks tremble, evaporating in a gold mist. When night falls, there remains a heat in the quiet water of the sea, that shines with the reflection of heavy, drowning, huge, low stars. The strange silhouettes of the giant thistles are outlined against the clarity of the sky, and in the heat they appear to be flames of green fire. There is no possible escape nor can one feel indifference. I know people, like myself, who love it, who love it violently and without reservation.[7]

One afternoon Marta in *The Island and the Devils* travels to the south of the Great Canary Island in search of Pablo, her artist friend:

In front of her, the dazzling lava beds ended in a background of mountains inflamed at dusk. Mountains that seemed unusual to Marta, of geometric shapes, flattened, strange, enveloped in a red and blue haze, as if the valleys were bonfires that spewed their brilliance and smoke upon them. Behind the little house the very wide cliff stretched out to the sea. Some dark forms, some clustered huts could be seen at a distance, near the water. The only vegetation were those enormous thistles, wild teasels, larger than the largest rocks. They looked like green fires amidst the blackness of the terrain. The ground gave off heat. And the strip of water, at a distance, gave an impression of serenity, sadness, and reverie.[8]

Thus Laforet incorporates personal spatial experience into the novelistic construct. Marta is traveling alone for the first time, and, although she is brave and adventuresome, the world is large and overwhelming. She has precociously overstepped the bounds of decorum for a Spanish girl her age, and the southern landscape thus described evokes the dangers that await her in such a breach.

More even than landscapes and a sense of geographical place, Laforet is adept at capturing quadrangular space—a street (often narrow) or the interior of a room. She is always aware of herself as coinciding in space, of sharing a place with streets and buildings. For this reason it is so important to her to live in the quaint Trastevere section of Rome, a place with history, interesting houses, and vitality. Many of her journal articles conjure up spaces familiar to her Spanish journal readership. For example, in an article entitled "La casa" (The House), Laforet talks of the sensation of living in a house of the style found in Spanish villages. Most city-dwelling Spaniards now live in huge apartment buildings:

I had forgotten nonetheless, the feeling that a deep entry-way gives with its bright doorbell that lets one hear the little bell in the distant interior when it is pressed. When the door opens, there comes the sensation of finding a stone patio with a stone well in the center and then the huge rooms. . . . Air and sun enter the house and her best face is the one not seen from the street, it is the one that peers out to the countryside. In the house, upon opening the window to sleep, the clean night air comes in and finds large spaces and fills them without causing drafts, banging doors, or breaking anything. There are dark rooms for trunks, those rooms where children love to play and frighten each other; there are old paintings on the walls and clocks that harmoniously give the time. . . . And, above all, there is silence, a pure, pleasant, lively silence that does not issue from absence of life, but from the necessary space and from the solid thickness of the walls, a silence that even the maids do not interrupt when they are in the kitchen.[9]

Laforet's characters are always located in a particular space—Andrea *in* her grandmother's house, *in* Barcelona; Marta *in* her mother's estate house *in* the Canaries. Paulina shifts locations from León to Madrid, from *within* her mother-in-law's house to *within* her Madrid apartment. Each of these protagonists has a particular room with which she is associated, forming her personal space, a basis from which she reaches out to the world. Martín's room in *La insolación* (Sunstroke) is the scene of his fall or disgrace and thus is the locus that reflects his personal development. In talking about a *tertulia* (a regular social gathering of friends who share similar interests) that took place in her relative's house in Madrid in the early 1940s, Laforet says:

Neruda was with us. He arrived in a book, under the arm of one of the members of the group, and he almost never missed one of our meetings. . . . In that small room, with a window through which one could see the mountains, something as huge as the work of Neruda could fit.[10]

Walls contain and limit the human spirit, but they cannot dominate it, and on the positive side, they often provide the lens and filter through which the world is seen more clearly. The juxtaposition of the confining and defining characteristics of space is at the heart of Laforet's creation in the four long novels.

One way in which Laforet captures in her verbal art the space she has lived in or imagined is through an artist's description, a description that seems to imitate a certain style of painting. For example, the southern Canary village she described in a travel article (quoted above), when introduced into *The Island and the Devils*, becomes a verbal depiction of a Cézanne painting from his pre-Cubist period. The shapes are geometrical, the houses clustered and uniform, and there are no people; color and shape are the dominant features of the description. Laforet often moves her characters into a situation with a painter's description, just as she is capable of transporting herself in space through the use of iconographic aids:

In the folder of watercolors, I find the Boca District in Buenos Aires. Its damp atmosphere and the rose and blue of its wood houses are here. The trees, the mosquitoes, the smells of Percheron horses and the mud of the canals through which the Paraná empties into the Plata are present.[11]

One would hardly suspect she has never been to South America.

Several experiences involving Tangiers, which she recorded in her *ABC* column, are illustrative of the way in which Laforet's spatial memory and verbal art are mutually dependent. One example comes from a factual travel article:

Often when I am in Tangiers, I go up to the highest point of Alcazaba Hill to the Riad Sultan Café. For me, Tangiers is a city full of peaceful corners, full of scenes of tranquil beauty, where the sea nearly always shows through the trees or between the white walls; it is a religious city where one hears the call of Catholic church bells, and there are mosques, synagogues and Protestant temples as well. All exist side by side amidst this life of open sea and sky, above the life of the port. Amidst the commercial hubbub of her streets, this burst of depth, this feeling of time lived drop by drop, in silence; there is no desire to kill time, but to enjoy it simply in silence, as the people of this land do.[12]

In another article, Laforet describes how her memory of the city, comprehended directly with the five senses, fuses with other images and stimuli in a dream. During the dream (which occurs in her Madrid apartment), she is in the Tangiers café described in the travel article:

Then it all disappears [as she awakens], but in the dark room in Madrid, I continue remembering the city of Tangiers and I have the impression that I have dreamt many of its environments as a continuation of the last reading of the evening before.[13]

She had been reading *California Trip* by Allen Ginsburg and so begins to search for a connection between Tangiers and the "beat" poets (whom she mistakenly calls the "beatles"). Then she remembers that Ginsburg had lived in Tangiers shortly before her last visit there and had told some of her friends of his new method for attempting to find the exact words to express pure sensation. He sat in a bath of constant temperature with his eyes and ears covered, a slow, monotonous metronome apparatus on his head, and a paper and pencil at hand. He was trying to lull to sleep the brain cells man normally uses and to awaken those that are not normally used. Once relaxed, Ginsburg would see images and memories of secondary, forgotten things: faces in the streets, corners, moments, sometimes precious emotions. He wrote of the impression of these images that had lain dormant until then, of feeling reborn, with extraordinary freshness. Some of these images, memories, and sensations formed the basis of the poem "Howl". Laforet describes her subconscious process in this incident:

It is as if my dream that night had been provoked by an experience of the new poetry. From the reading of a bit of "Howl," I have been carried to the memory of Tangiers with the luminous sea breaking on the cliff below the old café that Alexander Dumas frequented on his trips. . . .[14]

This experience is a microcosm of Laforet's artistic process: observation and experience come first, then memory fuses with art to produce the new vision, her own personal vision, the one revealed in her books. The plastic arts (a building or a painting) frequently serve as stimuli to memory in this process. Her use of artistic descriptions has a dual purpose: to aid a character's memory and to emphasize the function of art in life. That her main characters are often artists or are associated with artists is a clue to one of the principal aims and achievements of her work: to explore the nature of artistic sensitivity and to understand the creative process itself. In the discussion of *Nothing*, I will detail Laforet's novelistic use of the visual arts.

IV   *Autobiography*

As I discuss the novels and stories in later chapters there will be a great temptation to see Carmen Laforet's life in them, particularly in her heroines, who are women in search of themselves, in her treatment of familial relations, and even in her secondary characters, who seem to have much in common with her friends. Laforet has emphatically denied that she or her friends are her characters; she denies that she is Andrea of *Nothing* or Marta of *The Island and the Devils*, that Linka is portrayed in Ena, Andrea's best friend in *Nothing*, or that her family is depicted in her novelistic families. Of course, what any writer writes is his or her own life in some way; it logically must be the distillation and artistic recreation of personal experience. Sometimes the fictional incarnations of these experiences resemble identifiable real-life people and sometimes they do not. But whatever their origin or resemblance, they owe their existence and life to the fictional world that has been created to surround them and not to the real world. This I think is what Laforet objects to—the suggestion that what she writes is like history or journalism, that art has not intervened in her novelistic creations.

It is helpful to consider the example of Proust in this matter. No one would deny that Proust is a great novelist; he is not a great writer of autobiography. Nor would anyone deny that the correlation between Proust's own life and the fictional lives in his novels is extremely high. The key to distinguishing between autobiography and fiction in Proust or in any author is the art employed; in novel-writing the principal artistic medium is the narrative technique.

The narration introduces the distancing and focusing mechanism by which the reader is maintained in the fictional world. In some cases, as in *Remembrance of Things Past* and *Nothing*, the authorial personality (in Wayne Booth's sense of a unifying world-view that defines the taste and morality implied in the work—not the real author, be it Proust or Laforet) and the narrator (person or voice telling the story) are the same; these fictions are autobiographical. According to Louis Rubin, the term autobiography may be used to apply to fiction when "the authorial personality becomes the point of temporal focus upon which the meaning of the fiction centers, and the meaning lies in his memories."[15]

Memory for Laforet is the point of transition between life and art; she understands that time and memory are the material and the distancers in the artistic process:

The song of a bird, a drop of water that for a moment had all the colors of the rainbow in it, continues in my memory, and perhaps for years will reside in this mortal organism that is my body, and perhaps forever enrich my immortal soul.[16]

In art, memory alone is not enough; imagination must mold and shape memory. She comments after seeing a documentary film of the early part of this century in which film clips, photographs, and testimonials were used:

Our age is going to be profusely illustrated. Historians of the future will have a valuable archive of smiles, gestures, and voices of famous people. . . . But without a prodigious imagination, will they be able to reconstruct them as they are for us now? I do not think so. I believe that memory has to be transmitted from generation to generation by passing through the sensitivity of intermediary creators. The concerns of man should be told to new generations by sensitive, creative men capable of taking in details, vibrations, and shades that a camera with all its objectivity can never give us, because it is not the gesture of the man that counts but the spirit of the gesture.[17]

This then is Laforet's attitude toward her vocation as a writer of fiction: she is an observer, rememberer, and artistic interpreter. Discussing realistic fiction in one of her articles, Laforet denies the possibility of artistic "realism," by comparing realistic writing to photography:

Nothing more realistic than a photograph, right? But take a close-up of a face and see what happens: a pore that was fortunately invisible to the naked eye is converted into a volcano. . . . To describe some human beings in a few lines is not difficult for a novelist, but it is risky if one is attempting a portrait. . . . I have never done a portrait of anyone.[18]

No matter how lifelike (autobiographical or truthful) a piece of fiction may seem, it should never be considered as anything but art, and, by the same token, the fiction writer should not lose sight of his role as a transformer and not a copier of reality.

V *Feminism*

The plots of Laforet's novels do not seem to have much form, but on careful examination it is clear that they subtly move the reader toward an understanding and appreciation of the characters' psychology and motivations. The four novels published to date and many of the stories, although each has very different characters and life situations, share a basic theme or paradigm. The protagonist is presented in one set of social and psychological circumstances, from which he or she attempts to escape. After contact with the "outside world" or at least a different world from his or her own, the protagonist encounters a solution to his drive to find his appropriate place in life. Margaret E. W. Jones interprets this basic paradigm as a feminist approach to the life situation:

The dissatisfaction with social reality . . . [is] present in Laforet's books through several sets of dialectical pairs which offer an implicit critical view by revealing the distance between personal aspiration and the hostility with which such plans are met. For example, the struggle for physical as well as spiritual independence clashes against the restrictions imposed on the protagonist; second, contrasting character pairs who act as potential role models underline the intensity of the confrontation. Finally certain stylistic elements transmit the dual view of life, using descriptive distortion to substantiate the protagonist's feeling of alienation. The choice of the dialectical viewpoint enhances the feminist theme because the ideological tension it predicates complements the emotional disorientation of the character.[19]

Laforet actually sees the conflict between individual aspirations and social limitation on the individual as a universal dilemma; the same

paradigm functions in *Sunstroke* with a male protagonist. It only
appears to be a female problem in the total literary creation of
Carmen Laforet, because the majority of her protagonists are
women or girls.

The theme of all four of Laforet's novels is the rite of passage,
a growing awareness on the part of the protagonist of his or her
identity and how he or she fits into society. The family, its members,
its setting, and the interaction of these elements form the microcosm
in which the rite takes place. Carmen Laforet, together with Camilo
José Cela (author of *La familia de Pascual Duarte*, the first novel
published after the Civil War), is a pioneer in using the family as
a paradigm to depict the ills of modern Spain. This use of the family
in the post–Civil War Spanish novel has now become one of the
most significant features of that important body of fiction.

In scaling down the importance of feminist issues (problems peculiar to women) in Laforet's fiction, I would not wish to exclude
feminism from the concerns of her writing or from her interests as
a human being. Surely there is a sensitivity in her work to the
restrictions placed on and the frustrations encountered by women,
especially when they step beyond the traditional roles of housewife
and mother. Some of the most astute criticism of Laforet's works
uses a feminist approach. If the feminist motif is present in her
novels, however, it is as a leitmotif rather than a central theme; in
the discussion of individual novels, I point out, in passing, the way
in which the feminist motifs are incorporated into the larger spheres
of interest. Attesting to Laforet's personal concern for the place of
women not only in Spanish society, but universally, is the fact that
she has projected a book on the subject. In addition, approximately
20 percent of her newspaper articles deal with great women in
painting and literature or with subjects of interest primarily to
women (family and children), from what could be called a feminist
point of view.

Once she was asked in an interview whether she wrote because
she liked to or because she wished to affirm the worth of women.
This question reminded her that she awoke very late and very
gradually to the oppression many women suffer. She had grown up
in a family that made less of a distinction between the roles of the
male and female children than is traditional in Spanish families. It
never occurred to her that there were certain things a woman could
and could not write or that she should write in order to assert the

value of women. She did not realize until much later the frustrations and anguish some talented women feel, and in later years she has become quite interested in the phenomenon: "Until now I have never tried especially to express these problems in my narratives."[20] Discussing female writers in her newspaper columns, she treats them only as authors, rather than as women writers per se. But she does understand that a female artist envisions the world in a different way than does a man:

Nothing more feminine than the book of Susana March. . . . And I understand by feminine in this case the telluric feeling that all women carry within themselves to a certain degree, as if our spirit drew its loftiest sensations from the earth.[21]

In several articles she tackles the prejudice against women's power of creative fantasy. In answer to Mercedes Ballesteros's suggestion in a lecture that women ought to stay away from novel-writing because they lack fantasy, Laforet counterattacks that current Spanish male novelists have become bogged down in the realistic mode. And she reacts to Rafael Vázquez Zamora's assertions that women cannot be creative, that genius in a woman would be monstrous, and that there could never be a female Balzac or Faulkner, by saying that she admires many contemporary female novelists more than Faulkner, "in spite of the fact that his intelligence shines with brilliant sparks, among the whole tiresome parade of his novels, deliberately confused and forcedly horrible."[22] She prefers Selma Lagerlof, Virginia Woolf, Margaret Kennedy, and Milli Dandalo to perhaps the most important novelist of the twentieth century after Proust and Joyce, but one should remember (in fairness) that this opinion was expressed in the early 1950s when Faulkner was not well understood in Spain. Also, at this time, Carmen Laforet was viewing the world through the eyes of a rather zealous recent Catholic convert; Faulkner's seeming lack of charity toward humankind could not have appealed to her then. In the same *Destino* column a month later (perhaps due to recriminations from readers) she reveals more about her prejudice against Faulkner. She experiences discomfort, not so much with the horror of his books, but with his style; her words tell as much about herself as they do of the other novelist. She misses a sense of space in Faulkner: "We never know if [the characters] are in a room or are in the open countryside . . . all the weighty world of walls and doors that logically have to be opened and closed disappears."[23]

In writing of a lecture by Lili Álvarez, who asserts that true femininity is a sacrifice, Laforet remains suspiciously objective in presenting the other woman's ideas: "I do not pretend to have completely captured the idea of the speech given by Mrs. Álvarez. . . ."[24] The protagonist of *The New Woman* seems to suggest this sacrificial idea of womanhood, but the treatment of the theme in that novel is ambiguous, as is Laforet's attitude toward other human problems she treats fictionally. Perhaps Laforet's greatest contribution to feminism is that she is a fine novelist who happens to be a woman, and as such has helped to open the way for a proliferation of female novelists in the post–Civil War period, among them Ana María Matute, Elena Quiroga, Dolores Medio, Carmen Martín Gaite, and Ana María Moix.

Carmen Laforet's fiction has a prophetic quality about it, and so it seems appropriate to end these general chapters on her life and work with the words of a kind of fortune-teller. Matilde Ras, a well-known handwriting analyst and a close personal friend of Laforet, saw her primary characteristics as perfectionism, independence, and claustrophobia. Matilde Ras also observed that Laforet has more of a visual than auditory orientation and has a tendency to depression, though appearing outwardly cheerful. Her life and her books bear out these observations to a remarkable degree.

CHAPTER 3

Nada *(Nothing)*

I *Introduction*

B ECAUSE it is her best and her most widely read work, both
in Spain and abroad, *Nada* (Nothing), Carmen Laforet's first
novel, requires a chapter to itself. *Nothing* has attracted more critical attention than all the rest of Laforet's writing together, and it
has the greatest number of translations and editions, including a
condensed and annotated classroom edition for English-speaking
students.[1] (I will return to this edition later in the chapter.) The
diversity of the interpretations is evidence of the richness and ambiguity of the novel. And because of the ambiguity, the various
interpretations, including proto-Catholic, feminist, mechanistic,
and existential, are not mutually exclusive.

The title itself projects ambiguity. Almost on the strength of the
title alone, the novel has often been called existentialist; its appearance at the height of the existentialist movement in France
encourages this interpretation. The title also suggests the residue
of despair and devastation left in Spain after the Civil War. The
violent scenes and the depiction of hunger have led critics to classify
Nothing as *tremendista*, a type of literature peculiar to the Spanish
1940s in which acts of seemingly unmotivated violence are the basis
of the plot. Laforet herself has said that her primary purpose in
writing the novel was to recapture the ambience of post–Civil War
Barcelona in the early 1940s. She accomplished this goal, and, in
the process, wrote a novel of great thematic and narrative complexity.

Nothing is prefaced by a fragment of a poem of the same title by
Juan Ramón Jiménez, one of Spain's leading twentieth-century
poets:

> At times, a bitter taste,
> An unpleasant odor, a strange

> Light, a discordant tone,
> A touch that ennervates,
> Reaches our senses
> Like fixed realities
> And appears to us to be
> The unexpected truth... (*Novelas*, p. 21)

The meaning of these lines is twofold, suggesting two levels of meaning in the novel. The "bitter taste and discordant tone" could refer to a pessimistic view of life's realities—in the novel, the unpleasant social, economic, and political situation in Spain immediately after the Civil War. But the poem is really not about the exterior historical or biographical events of life; rather, it suggests how we gain knowledge or understanding of the world latently as a distillation of experience. *Nothing* depicts the same process.

The theme of the acquisition of knowledge and awareness is imbedded in the narrative voice. In *Nothing*, Carmen Laforet's only first-person narrative, the narrator is the protagonist speaking when she is several years older than the eighteen-year-old Andrea, who experiences a year of life with relatives while attending the University of Barcelona. This temporal dichotomy between narration and experience is the key to the fundamental and most durable effect of the book—to portray the crucial stage of development in the life of the adolescent, his (her) passage from late childhood to incipient adulthood, particularly his growing awareness of self. In the process we are introduced to some well-drawn characters and are immersed in the ambience of Barcelona's streets and architecture and enmeshed in the underlying political dichotomy of modern Spain.

II   *Andrea's World*

The orphan Andrea arrives in Barcelona at night and leaves a year later in the morning. This shift symbolizes two important elements in the novel—Andrea's heightened sense of self and the two worlds in which she has lived for a year, worlds that have helped her shape her own destiny. Her family's world represents traditional Spain. They reside in half of a once-grand apartment, the other half of which they have sold along with much of the furniture and fine things. Andrea lives in this dark and musty place with her spinster aunt Angustias, two uncles (one married with a child), and their mother, Andrea's grandmother. M. Fernández Almagro has pointed out that each character in himself suggests the outline for another novel.[2]

The description of the house and family the night of Andrea's arrival sets the lugubrious tone for this part of Andrea's life:

What was in front of me was an entry lighted by one weak light bulb, fixed to one of the arms of a magnificent chandelier, filthy with cobwebs, which hung from the ceiling. A dark backdrop of pieces of furniture piled on top of each other as at moving time. And in the foreground a black and white speck of a little, old, decrepit woman, in a night shirt, with a shawl thrown over her shoulders. I wanted to believe that I had gotten the wrong apartment, but that dejected little lady preserved a kindly smile that was so sweet; I was sure it was my grandmother. (*N*, p. 25)

Andrea gradually learns the secrets of this bizarre, degenerate family.

Román, the unmarried uncle, a double agent during the Civil War, is even now engaged in shady, black-market dealings. He is swarthily good-looking, a talented musician, composer, and painter. Women are fascinated by him and so is Andrea for a time, until the perverse side of his nature touches her personally. Román delights in teasing and tantalizing his brother Juan and sister-in-law Gloria, causing frequent family arguments. Juan, a weak person, fancies himself a good painter and pretends to make his living by painting, but he is actually much less talented than Román, who has painted only sporadically in his life. It is revealed late in the novel that Gloria, who seems vain and stupidly self-centered, really supports Juan and their child with earnings from gambling at her sister's establishment in the *barrio chino*. The story of Cain and Abel, symbolizing the Spanish Civil War, is suggested in these two brothers.

Angustias, the old-maid aunt, stands for the conservative values of Spanish society in which the only alternative for women who do not marry is to enter a convent; this is what Angustias finally does, although her self-sacrifice is equivocal. The novel hints that she has long been in love with her boss, Don Jerónimo, even that she has had an affair with him; perhaps she enters a convent more in desperation over an impossible love affair than to protect decorum or family honor. Hypocrisy and self-delusion are among the attitudes toward life that Andrea will eventually reject. Angustias takes charge of Andrea as a mother, but she is stern and strict, lacking the compassion, warmth, or understanding essential to an adequate mother figure. The old grandmother represents the extreme traditionalist position, but her tendency to bury all problems in religion is less obnoxious than Angustias's use of religion. Her kindliness and senility lend her a benign air, but they also make her an ineffectual guide for young Andrea.

The action of the novel is developed in a mystery-story fashion, raising questions in the reader's mind about the characters and their activities, but many loose ends are left unresolved: What were Román and Juan actually doing during the War? What exactly is the relationship between Román and Gloria? What is the relationship between Román and Ena (Andrea's best friend)? This technique is effective for two reasons: it heightens dramatic tension and thereby increases reader interest in the novelistic action, which otherwise has little plot, and it adds to the sense that the reader is seeing the world through an adolescent's eyes. A person of that age would not be expected to have full cognizance of the types of relationships that take place in the adult world or of what it was actually like to have experienced the war firsthand.

The other world in which Andrea moves centers on Ena's family, a progressive, bourgeois set of people, whose blond hair and light, cheerful, music-filled house represent the opposite pole of dualistic Spain. Andrea and Ena become fast friends at the university, partly, the reader is led to suspect, because Ena wishes an entrée to Andrea's family. She becomes involved with Román, who ultimately commits suicide after Ena jilts him. Ena's actions seem to be motivated by a desire to avenge Román's cruelty to her mother, who was in love with Román in her youth. Thus the two worlds are linked through several characters: Ena's mother and Román, Ena and Román, and finally through Andrea, who moves in and out of both. Andrea in the end seems to shift permanently to the "modern" progressive group when she decides to live with Ena's family in Madrid and take a job with Ena's father's company while finishing her university studies. During her year in Barcelona, Andrea has several romantic encounters and begins to be aware of herself as a sexual entity, after a rather androgynous beginning. Thus Andrea matures at several levels during this crucial year in her life, which she at first seems naively to think bore her "nothing". She has been primarily an observer, witnessing anguish, death, love, and artistic endeavor, all of which will contribute to her more mature view of life in the future.

III   *Critical Interpretations of* Nothing

Sherman Eoff reads *Nothing* as a "venture in mechanistic dynamics." He believes the characters are projected as things in the world moved by mechanistic force and that psychological motivation is reduced to a minimum. Continuing the metaphor of physics he applies to the novel, Eoff says that "various characters, after whirring like atoms in an electric current, separate themselves from the area of disturbance or eventually explode."[3] While this aspect surely exists in the novel, it relates only to its most superficial structure; the psychological motivations are implicit, rather than explicit. Eoff arrives at a conclusion about the author's world that, while not existentialist per se, is compatible with the sense of lost faith and meaninglessness to which existentialism leads.

David William Foster, on the other hand, associates *Nothing* with the romance, a type of narrative which flourished in the late Middle Ages and in the Romantic period. He points out the Gothic aspect of the house on Aribau Street and its function as a microcosmic world from which the heroine sallies forth. He predicates his examination of the novel on the definition of romance given by Richard Chase, according to whom reality is rendered in "less volume and detail" than in the realistic novel of the nineteenth century and "tends to prefer action to character. . . . The romance can flourish without providing much intricacy of relation. The characters, probably rather two-dimensional types, will not be completely related to each other or to society or to the past."[4] Both Foster and Eoff base their interpretations on the elliptical, hermetic nature of Laforet's narrative technique, failing to take into consideration some important subtle hints to the psychological and sociological interpretations latent in the novel.

In signaling Andrea's three-stage development within a dual world, Foster points the way to the archetypal and mythic interpretation of the novel that has yielded some fine recent studies. Juan Villegas in his *La estructura mítica del héroe*[5] uses *Nothing* as an example of mythic structure in the contemporary novel. According to this pattern, the mythic hero's (or heroine's) life trajectory is seen as a quest, which begins with a first part, or leave-taking (separation from home and family), to go in search of freedom and personal identity through a series of adventures in a hostile environment. In this quest the hero is aided by a series of "fairy godmothers" in the guise of friends (in *Nothing*: Ena, Ena's family, Pons) and is controlled by a protective person (Angustias). The second part, centering on the themes of love and friendship, is the initiation into and practice of the newfound liberation. In *Nothing* this phase begins with the departure of Angustias. The labyrinth motif common to mythic literature is introduced through Andrea's bohemian wanderings about Barcelona, and the necessary "descent into Hell" is represented by her mad dash through the red-light district in pursuit of Juan. The third part contains the end of the initiation and the affirmation of the self; here friendship intervenes again to aid Andrea. Through Ena she attains her job, education, and living in Madrid—the eventual means to her self-fulfillment.

Elizabeth Ordóñez enriches this reading of *Nothing* by adding a feminist and sociological perspective. Ordóñez emphasizes the importance of the family paradigm in the novel's meaning and structure in her interpretation of it as a reflection of Spain's post–Civil War political and social values:

[Laforet] manipulates the choices of her protagonist in such a way so as to insure that Andrea enter into and experience a negative form of the family (according to ideal patriarchal, bourgeois values), and then abandons that context in order to move concurrently outward and *into* a positive familial structure (again according to the standards of an implied, ideal set of measurements). This final initiation and integration is thus in turn a function of a larger societal construct, the patriarchal society as a whole. . . .[6]

While Ordóñez's feminist perspective reflects dubious optimism upon her conclusion that Andrea is guided toward a final entry into patriarchal bourgeois society, Michael Thomas believes that *Nothing* projects a positive view of Andrea's development. According to Professor Thomas, Andrea undergoes a positive learning experience in each phase of her year in Barcelona, signaled by respective recognition scenes occurring symbolically near a door (passageway).[7] Certainly the novel can be read and persuasively argued to be either positive or negative, optimistic or pessimistic, in terms of Andrea's experience in Barcelona and the resolution of that experience in the move to Madrid, but the division in the criticism points perhaps to an unresolvable ambiguity of the novel.

Sara Schyfter adds another dimension to the feminist perspective in her paper "The Male Mystique in Carmen Laforet's *Nada*." She analyzes the male and female role models available to Andrea in her developing awareness of sexuality. In this process Román represents the negative, dangerous side of the male's attraction for the female, the aspect of male/female relations that precludes development and fulfillment of the woman. Professor Schyfter points out that Román touches the life of every woman in the novel, affecting each in a negative way: "With Román's death, a new type of human interaction is now possible between the sexes, a relationship like that of Jaime and Ena."[8]

When *Nothing* was published in 1944, it was hailed as a fresh, new direction in Spanish fiction, but most of the interpretations discussed above concentrate on themes and world-view rather than on narrative techniques. Ruth El Saffar's insightful article "Structural and Thematic Tactics of Suppression in Carmen Laforet's *Nada*" is one of the few studies[9] to concentrate on narrative technique. El Saffar signals the discrepancy between "the young girl who arrives in Barcelona at the beginning of the work and the self into which she has matured as she undertakes to recount the story of the year she has spent there."[10] This discrepancy allows two somewhat opposing world-views to operate in the book: that of an innocent young girl who optimistically believes in a better life ahead and the authorial perspective which reveals a lack of such hope. In her interpretation El Saffar contradicts the interpretations that see personal development in Andrea during her year in Barcelona; for El Saffar, there is change, but it occurs between the time Andrea leaves Barcelona and the time she writes her story. The change is presented through the narrative technique. The pessimistic undercurrent present in the authorial voice is supported by the themes of decay and the impotence of art to delay the erosion of time that run through the book. El Saffar finds a bridge between the authorial "I" and the younger girl only at the end of the novel when Andrea is going off to a new life in Madrid, where she will meditate on her year in Barcelona. But actually there is a continual bridging of the two levels through manipulations of verb tenses, creating a dialectic between the "then" and the "now." Thus the process of creation or recreation in memory becomes the focal point of the novel. *Nothing* is (in the sense discussed above) an autobiographical exploration of personal artistic awakening and development.

IV   *The Role of Art in* Nothing

The eighteen-year-old Andrea, upon whose experiences during a year in Barcelona the novel is based, is a future artist, a writer. Within the novelistic action, she never writes so much as a letter, but her vocation as a novelist is built into the narrative voice. Carmen Laforet has not understood the complexity of her own narrative medium. She says in the introduction to *Nothing*:

When I wrote the novel I had many impressions accumulated in solitude and an instinctive wisdom: that of realizing that if it were true that I could see and feel certain things that my sensitivity accepted or rejected, I did not have the experience to judge them. For that reason I put the narrative in the mouth of a young girl, who is practically a ghost narrating.(*N*, p. 17)

The perceiver in the novel is "a young girl," but the person who narrates is older and wiser, making us constantly aware that what we are being told is an interpretation. The time lapse between the events and their recounting could have been deemphasized, but Laforet has chosen to use many narrative devices that heighten rather than diminish the distance. There are actually three narrative time levels functioning in the novel: (1) the narrator's present, indicated by a rare present-tense verb; (2) the narrrator's past, her year in Barcelona, chronologically told and often prefaced by "I remember that" to stress the dual temporality; and (3) flashbacks within the chronological narration introduced by "I was remembering" or "I remembered." The second level predominates, but the first narrative level appears often enough to remind the reader that time has elapsed between the events and their reconstruction— the time necessary for artistic recreation.

Creating a work of art, in fact, becomes a way of understanding the world for the narrator; it has an epistemological function. She explores her growing sensory awareness of the world, and her sensitivity seems to emerge primarily through contact with the visual and spatial arts, much like that of Stephen Dedalus in James Joyce's *A Portrait of the Artist as a Young Man*. Finally she expresses her

impressions in words or literature—her own artistic means of capturing her experiences. Many of her attempts to recreate her past
have recourse to plastic techniques, so that art has multiple functions
in the novel: (1) it is an important part of the education of the
developing artistic sensitivity, (2) it helps Andrea recreate her experience, and (3) it is the final product of all these processes. Art
(or recollected experience) and real life are in constant conflict
throughout the novel, but art wins out in the end. The finished
product is a work of art, not a slice of life.

To achieve the artistic distance, the frame and perspective of the
scenes she depicts from her year in Barcelona, Andrea keeps us
temporally removed from the action by a cloudy glass, the filter of
her memory of past events. One of the ways in which the mature
Andrea conveys the highly subjective nature of her report is to
preface many of her memories with a sense verb: "I heard a trem-
bling voice . . ."; "I saw that grandmother . . ."; or she begins the
sentence with "It seemed to me that. . . ." The instances of more
objectively worded descriptions are relatively rare. Even when a
scene takes place without its narration filtering through Andrea's
senses, she manages to make herself, rather than the thing described, the center of attention:

My aunt's room was adjacent to the dining room and had a balcony on the
street. She was seated at her little desk with her back to me. I stopped to
look at the room, astonished, because it appeared clean and in order, as
though it were a separate world from the rest of the house. There was a
mirrored wardrobe closet and a large crucifix covering another door that
led to the entryway; at the side of the head of the bed was a telephone.
(*N*, p. 34)

The phrase "I stopped," placed squarely in the middle of this otherwise objective description, makes Andrea the focal point of the
scene; the objects described appear to depend upon her.

Other characters' comments about Andrea constitute a major
source of doubts as to the reliability of her perceptions. The comments generally contradict or conflict with impressions of herself
that Andrea has given. For example, she enjoys Román's music and
several times indicates that she believes him to be a musical genius,
but he denigrates her musical taste, saying: "No. You do not have
an ounce of musical culture, that is why you judge me thus" (*N*, p.

89). Román mentions other characteristics of a girl her age that
would cause us to mistrust her judgment:

Look, I wanted to talk to you, but it is impossible. . . ."what I feel like
doing"... that is all you have in your head with the clarity of a child.
Sometimes I think you are like me, that you understand me, that you
understand my music, the music of the house... (*N*, p. 89)

Physical weakness impairs her rational powers and even her ability to see clearly. After Angustias leaves, and she gains control of
her own finances, she often spends her entire orphan's allowance
the first few days of the month and then nearly starves for weeks,
with consequent negative effects for her perceptions: "Through
Antonia I also found out the last details of Román's life. Details that
I heard as through a mist. (It seemed to me that I was losing the
faculty of seeing well. That the edges of things were becoming
fuzzy)" (*N*, p. 247). And, of course, there is the fundamental human
problem of sorting out reality from fiction, even when one's physical
condition is normal: "Nonetheless, Gloria's steps decided brusquely
to head downstairs toward the street. All this was so strange that
I attributed it to my imagination running wild" (*N*, p. 89). Andrea,
the mature narrator, often points out mistakes in her earlier perceptions: "I judged her [Angustias] without any compassion, as not
very bright and as authoritarian. I have made so many mistaken
judgments in my life that I am still not certain that that one is
correct" (*N*, p. 36).

The reader begins to wonder how accurate any of the narration
is. Perhaps all the events are purely reconstructed figments of the
mature Andrea's imagination: "Who could understand the thousand
threads that unite the souls of men and the outreach of words? Not
a girl like I was then" (*N*, p. 188). The mature self is constantly
undermining the truth of the very material it seeks to have us
believe. We can never be sure that the judgments about her own
life and that of others are not just mature reflections on earlier
events, something she later reads into what happened to her previously, or if they were actually evaluations that she made at the
time of the event. In the following passage, the two verbs in the
imperfect ("did not like," "felt") give the impression that Andrea's
judgments occur simultaneously with the action, but the imperfect
(a tense which has no simple equivalent in English) also signifies

that the narrator is talking about something in the past and that time for reflection has elapsed:

I realized that he thought I was a different person: much more mature, perhaps more intelligent and certainly hypocritical and full of strange desires: I did not like to disillusion him, because I vaguely felt myself inferior, a little dull with my dreams and my sentimentalism, that I tried to hide in front of those people. (*N*, p. 47)

The reader is always aware, perhaps subconsciously, from the verbtense clue that Andrea might not have formulated these opinions so logically and firmly at the time she was experiencing the situation, but has in the interim organized and analyzed. From the point of view of a mere retelling of a series of events, which is what any novel is, this feature would appear to make little difference, but when considered in the light of objective versus artistic truth it is fundamental.

When Andrea says that Román "stretched out on the bed, smoking, his features relaxed as if time had no value, as if he had lain down to die smoking" (*N*, p. 47), the foreshadowing (however innocently presented) of Román's death belies her innocence as a narrator. She denies her innocence on other occasions in allowing herself a generalization or deductive comment about her entire year on Aribau Street when the year has only begun: "The impression of feeling myself drawn to his congeniality that I had felt when he talked to me for the first time, never returned" (*N*, p. 47). Or she reveals something learned later, casting a more complete picture of an immediate situation than would otherwise be possible: "Later I saw his [Pujol's] paintings, which he did by imitating point by point the defects of Picasso—of course, genius cannot be reproduced" (*N*, p. 142). Is this the voice of the mature or eighteen-year-old Andrea? Which one of the two thinks that Pujol's paintings are poor and that Picasso (with all of his defects) is a genius?

Even more ethereal are the narrator's recollections of dreamed or imagined scenes. The dreams and daydreams are stills from her album of memories that have come to form imaginary paintings in her mind. The picture of Gloria in the arms of Juan, when he visits her in the hospital at the end of the war, is a recurring image: "I closed my eyes and I saw a reddish darkness behind my eyelids. Then came the image of Gloria in the clinic, very white, leaning against Juan's shoulder; he was different, tender and did not have those gray shadows on his cheeks..." (*N*, p. 59). Pons's party is described almost entirely in set pieces: "A fat lady is frozen in my memory, her face congested with a smile at the moment she is raising a pastry to her mouth. I do not know why I have this image eternally suspended amidst the confusion and movement of all the others" (*N*, p. 196).

The most subjective of all descriptions are those in which the exterior reality is actually transformed into a work of art, a painting in a clearly recognizable style. The two styles she cultivates primarily are Expressionism and Impressionism, which in turn reflect the polarity of Andrea's life: the dark side (Calle de Aribau) and the light side (the university and Ena's family), respectively. Andrea herself implicitly recognizes the painter's symbology: "These streams of light that my life received thanks to Ena, were embittered by the somber cast which stained my spirit the other days of the week" (*N*, p. 129). The first night she enters the strange house on Aribau Street she transforms the bathroom into an Expressionist vision of somber colors and twisted shapes:

What pale, green light there was throughout the house: The low ceiling full of cobwebs was reflected in the spotted mirror over the basin, and my own body among the bright streams of water, was trying not to touch those filthy walls, standing on tiptoes above the porcelain bathtub.

That bathroom seemed like a witch's house. The soiled walls preserved the mark of clenched hands, of shouts of despair. Everywhere the chipped places opened their toothless mouths, oozing moisture. Above the mirror, because there was no other place for it, was hung a macabre still-life of pale fish and onions on a black background. Insanity smiled in the twisted faucets. (*N*, pp. 28–29)

Barcelona's rich architecture and unique neighborhoods lend themselves to Laforet's artistic transformation. Andrea's midnight dash down the Ramblas in pursuit of Juan is another excellent example of Expressionist distortion:

A river of lights ran down Pelayo Street. The advertisements winked their eyes in a boring game. . . . The people really were grotesque: a man passed to the side of me, his eyes laden with mascara under his wide hat. His cheeks were rosy. (*N*, pp. 157, 159)

The Expressionist visions often occur when Andrea is about to enter or has just come in contact with a new world: the house on Aribau

Street, the *barrio chino*, Pons's house. The wild, fantastic imagination of Gaudi's Expressionistic architecture seems to penetrate
some of Andrea's memories: "That Christmas day, the street had
the look of an immense pastry shop, full of delectable things" (*N*,
p. 76).

The intense play of natural light typical of Impressionism (as
opposed to the artificial light of night that often characterizes
Expressionism) is evident in the happier moments of Andrea's year
in Barcelona. Representative of this phase are her Sundays on the
beach with Ena and Jaime, or this scene on the wharf:

I was at the port. The boxed-in sea presented its spots of brilliant oil to my
eyes; the odor of pitch, of rope, penetrated deeply in me. The ships were
huge with their extremely high sides. At times, the water seemed to shiver
like a fish shaking its tail; a little boat, the sound of an oar. There I was,
that summer's midday. From some ship's deck, perhaps some Nordic blue
eyes would see me as a minuscule brush stroke on a foreign stamp . . . I,
a Spanish girl, with dark hair, pausing for a moment on the wharf of the
port of Barcelona. In a few minutes life would continue and would move
me toward some other point. I would find myself with my body framed by
some other scenery. (*N*, p. 226)

Here she is actually imagining herself to be a painting in someone
else's mind.

This passage is reminiscent of a section in Proust's *Within a Budding Grove* in which Marcel, traveling by train, sees a peasant girl
from a window when they make a brief stop at a mountain village.
He sees her for a moment, and then she moves away, and the train
speeds on, but the moment of time becomes recorded in memory.
Like Marcel in that incident, Andrea, the mature narrator, uses the
moment by the wharf to draw a general conclusion about life: "In
a few minutes life would continue and move me toward some other
point." The mature narrator is giving order and meaning to an event
that in the normal course of life's events would have no significance,
and in this way we are subtly made aware of the authorial personality's presence.

The Surrealistic mode is suggested in the several dreams which
Andrea describes in symbolic visual images:

That night I had a very clear dream in which an old and obsessive image
was repeated: Gloria leaning on Juan's shoulder, was crying. . . . Little by

little, Juan underwent strange transformations. I saw him enormous and
dark with the enigmatic physiognomy of Xochipilli [a pre-Columbian god
figurine belonging to Román]. Gloria's pale face began to animate and to
revive. Xochipilli smiled too. Suddenly I recognized his smile: it was the
white, and slightly savage smile of Román. It was Román who was em-
bracing Gloria and the two were laughing. They were not in the clinic, but
in the countryside. It was a countryside with purple lilies, and Gloria's hair
was being blown by the wind. (N, p. 61)

The purple lilies refer to a painting Román did of Gloria during the
war; thus we have a painting within a paintinglike dream.

Román considers the god-statuette Xochipilli to be bad luck; like
other primitive works of art, it is endowed by its owner with magical
powers. Perhaps something of that magical function remains in the
modern use of art; it aids in recalling the most ephemeral aspects
of life—the emotion of a fleeting moment. The mature Andrea uses
art to help her formulate and recapture past experience. One of the
scenes which she has much difficulty remembering (an important
dialogue between Gloria and the grandmother) she sets down in the
form of a play—her kind of art (literature).

Specific painters and paintings are evoked in Andrea's gallery of
memories. The first night of her arrival, so important in her initiation
into the dual world that Barcelona will become for her, she sees
her bizarre family arranged at the door to greet her in a fashion
reminiscent of Picasso's blue-period paintings of families and cou-
ples with melancholy, elongated, emaciated bodies and faces:

[There were] several phantom-like women. . . . a dog . . . black, too [like
the maid's outfit] as though he were an extension of her mourning. . . . a
thin, young woman with her red hair awry above her sharp, white face,
languid, like a hanging sheet, heightening the sad projection of the
group. . . . all those figures seemed to me equally elongated and somber.
Elongated, quiet, and sad, like the candles in a village wake. (N, pp. 26–27)

Goya's black period is indicated once directly and several times
stylistically. For example, Andrea's extended family, which descends on the house on Aribau Street after Román's suicide, is
described as "faces that are hooked or flattened like a 'Capricho' by
Goya. Those mourners seemed to be celebrating a strange witch's
Sabbath" (N, p. 250–251). Goya's *Coloso*, representing the specter
of war over Spain and Europe as a monstrous human figure, is

conjured up in Andrea's imagination when she overhears two Catalan businessmen discussing profits to be made in the Second
World War: "A smile came to my lips as though I actually saw them
mounted in the red afternoon sky on the shoulders of a black phan-
tom of war that flew over the battlegrounds of Europe (with conical
magicians' hat on their important heads)..." (*N*, p. 198).

And Andrea's self-portraits resemble Picasso's *The Girl Before
the Mirror*, a painting in which the mirror image is not a repro-
duction of the "real" girl, but a strange, unexpected transformation.
The first time Andrea is before a mirror, in the bathroom the night
of her arrival in Barcelona, she describes everything *except* what
is in the mirror. In subsequent encounters with the reflecting object,
the image is acknowledged and described with increasing detail.
Andrea describes her mirrored portrait for the first time the day
Angustias announces she is leaving for the convent. Symbolically,
Angustias's leave-taking signals the end of one phase in Andrea's
life and the beginning of her greater self-awareness. Andrea sees
herself twice in mirrors the day of Pons's party, a significant moment
of self-discovery. But these are partial and distorted pictures of
herself; she is always surprised by what she sees. After Román's
suicide she sees herself for the last time in the bathroom mirror,
the same mirror that gave no reflection or that gave one she chose
to ignore the day she arrived. This last image is stark and realistic:
"I saw myself reflected in the mirror, miserably thin, and with my
teeth chattering as though I were dying of cold" (*N*, p. 246). The
self-image has developed from nothing, has passed through a stage
of distortion and has finally settled into a fairly accurate likeness.

Reflection in *Nothing* is both visual and conceptual. There is a
persistent parallel drawn between reflex in thought and reflex in
vision. For example, Ena's character, as revealed in her mistreat-
ment of Jaime, is suggested in a visual image:

It was impossible for me to believe in the beauty and truth of human
sentiments—as I with my eighteen years conceived of them then—when
I thought about all that Ena's eyes reflected (becoming radiant and laden
with sweetness, the look she only had when she was with Jaime) and how
it all vanished in a moment without leaving a trace. (*N*, p. 177)

Three reflective images fix the temporal distance of the story in the
final pages of the novel:

The child babbled in his highchair and I realized with astonishment that he had grown a great deal that year. The family lamp gave its reflection in the dark panes of the balcony window. (*N*, p. 258)

I went into Angustias's room for the last time. It was hot and the window was open, the familiar reflection of the street lamp spread over the stones in sad yellow streams. (*N*, p. 259)

The morning air was stimulating. The ground seemed damp with the night dew. Before getting into the car, I raised my eyes toward the house where I had lived for a year. The first rays of sun struck the window. A few moments later, Aribau Street and all Barcelona remained behind me. (*N*, p. 260)

The reflection of the rising sun on the window of the house where Andrea lived for a year symbolizes the darkness of that house, where light does not penetrate, and the somber life she is leaving. Her thoughts turn reflectively to that year in the final passage, which summarizes the three temporal levels of the novel: "I felt a lively emotion [level 2]. I was leaving now without having encountered anything that I had confusedly hoped for [level 3]: life in its plenitude, happiness, deep interest, love. I took nothing with me from that house on Aribau Street [level 2]. At least that is the way I saw things then [level 1]" (*N*, p. 260). The second time level, the year in Barcelona, ends with a "lively emotion"; the third time level, which takes place prior to the Barcelona year, is indicated in the hopes she had carried with her to the city, and the first level, the narrative present in Madrid, is suggested in the distancing abverb "then" and signals the insights gained by the mature narrator during the time that has elapsed since the events took place.

Andrea never spells out what she has come to believe she carries with her from that year, which at the time seemed to leave her with "nothing." She does not have to, because the diary becomes the material filling the vacuum of life, namely, memory transformed into art. Like any work of art *Nothing* is the evocation or recreation of images from past experience, set down in a particular medium as in Wordsworth's famous formula: "emotion recollected in tranquillity." Andrea is always making up stories about their family: "And don't go spinning novels: our arguments and our shouts have no cause, nor do they have an end... What have you begun to imagine about us? —I don't know. —I already know that you are always dreaming up stories about our characters" (*N*, p. 46). But despite the novel's hermetic truth (as it is told by Andrea), the reader is comfortable with the creation, precisely because he is aware of the creative act in the narrative voice. He accepts the uncertainties of Andrea's story because the mature Andrea's vision of it is an artistic whole that corroborates the taste of the authorial voice.

Art and memory in *Nothing* establish a symbiotic relationship. Not only is art memory and memory art, but art (outside the mind) aids memory. Art becomes the cause and effect in the novel. The complexity of this relationship is established the morning after Andrea's arrival. On that nightmarish occasion, the old wizened grandmother is a central figure. The first thing Andrea sees upon awakening the next morning is the grandmother transformed into a beautiful young bride. Not until she finishes describing the newly wedded couple does she reveal that this is a portrait hanging on the wall. Seeing the portrait stimulates her to daydream, recreating the first days of the grandmother's marriage in the then new and attractive house on Aribau Street. Another instance of the art/memory complex occurs when Andrea visits Guixols's studio after all the young "artists" have left for the summer; their paintings are "carefully covered with white cloths that seemed like ghosts wrapped in shrouds—souls of the memories of a thousand lively conversations" (*N*, p. 242).

Román's music, or the memory of it, is often a catalyst to Andrea's imagination. The important thing about Román's music is that it captures "the harmony and materiality of things" (*N*, p. 253), and it has (like all art) the property of leading the person out of himself:

At the moment in which he, standing in front of the fireplace, began to move the bow, I changed completely. My reservations disappeared, the light veneer of hostility against everyone that I had been forming. My soul, outstretched, like my own hands together, received the sound like the hard ground receives the rain. . . . And in waves there came to me first naive memories, dreams, struggles, my own vacillating present, then sharp joys, sadnesses, death, the feeling of my total desperation converted into beauty, painful harmony without light. (*N*, p. 48)

This is the first time Andrea equates art and *nothingness* in the novel, a parallel I will mention again later.

The interpretation of the inner life of the person through a work of art is best exemplified in the cathedral, where Andrea seeks solace on several occasions. She does not go to the cathedral for religious motives; she never enters the church. The exterior architecture, and especially the Gothic facade, are what attract her to the building. Art, architecture, and music are the threads that unify numerous disparate elements in the novel: it is a primary link between Andrea and Ena's families (Román and Ena's mother studied music together in the same conservatory, and Ena ostensibly visits Román to hear him play); the first time Andrea goes to the cathedral, she has just heard Ena's mother play and sing; before entering the bohemian world of Guixols's studio, Andrea and Pons visit the church of Santa María del Mar. In the last instance, the narrator juxtaposes the true, lasting art of the medieval church—art that has meaning for the human soul—and the superficial commercial art in which Guixols and his friends engage.

Characteristics of Andrea, the future artist, are reflected in all the artists in the novel: she is impractical like Juan; Ena says she has some of the bourgeois trappings of her family; and she feels at home with Pons's group; but she is most like Román. The grandmother, Ena, Don Jerónimo, and even Román himself remark on this similarity. Román is the most talented person in the novel; both he and Andrea are observers of others in a world of egocentric people. But only Román knows how to "give just the proper eloquence to the moment" (N, p. 253), exactly what Andrea will attempt to do in her book of memoirs.

Even while she is still in Barcelona, Andrea is already acquiring this same ability; she is gathering the distance and artistic vision that will be transformed into her book:

How many useless days! Days filled with stories, too many cloudy stories. Incomplete stories, scarcely initiated and already bloated like an old piece of wood left out in the weather. Stories that were too dark for me. Their odor, which was the rotten odor of my house, caused me a certain nausea. And nevertheless it had become the only interest of my life. Little by little I had begun to remain before my own eyes in a second level of reality, my senses open only for that life that buzzed in the apartment on Aribau Street. (N, p. 50)

Art provides a soothing, contemplative calm, a permanent reality in opposition to the passion and flux of human relationships. The use of paintinglike descriptions and other conscious artistic techniques merges with rather than detracts from the vitality of the work. The technique adds life to the novel by making us conscious of an artistic mind at work.

The principal difference between life and art is that life continues and becomes corrupt, while the work of art is permanent:

If that night—I thought—the world had ended, it would have remained completely closed and beautiful like a circle. That is the way things happen in the novels, in the movies; but in life... I was realizing for the first time that everything continues and becomes gray and is ruined in life, that there is no ending to our story until death comes and the body disintegrates... (*N*, p. 223)

As Ruth El Saffar shows, *Nothing* is a highly structured work of art; it closes a perfect circle, beginning at midnight and ending at sunrise.

Real life plays tricks on memories while art helps fix the meaningful moments:

I immediately had a nebulous perception, but at the same time vivid and fresh, as though it had been carried by the odor of a recently picked fruit, of what Barcelona was in my memory. . . . even the very journey of the day before from the station, which I added to my notion of the city, was something pale and false, artificially constructed like that which is too worked and handled and loses its original freshness. (*N*, p. 30)

All this now belonged to the past (it sometimes horrified me to think how the elements of my life appeared and dissolved forever, just when I had begun to consider them immutable). (*N*, p. 139)

After her year in Barcelona, Andrea has "a larger burden of memories on her shoulders" (*N*, p. 240). This is really her *nothing*, the "fixed realities" (in Juan Ramón's poem) that are finally the "unexpected truth" (also indicated in the poem). The first reference to *nothing* comes early in the novel, when Andrea is listening to Román's music:

And suddenly an enormous silence and then Román's voice: One could hypnotize you... What does the music tell you? Immediately my hands and soul closed up.
—Nothing, I don't know, only that I like it...

—It isn't true. Tell me what it says to you. What it says to you afterwards.
—Nothing.
He looked at me disillusioned a moment. Then while he put away his violin:
—No, it isn't true. (*N*, pp. 48–49)

In a sense they are both right. Literally the music does not *say* anything, but it contains everything—especially the power to evoke memory. And so, finally her year of life on Aribau Street becomes *Nothing*—a memory, Andrea's novel.

The theme of art is important in Laforet's other novels and in some of her stories, but not in the same way. She never again uses the narrative voice employed in *Nothing* that creates a compelling novelistic tension based on elliptical and hazy perceptions. In *Nothing* the final truth is left to the imagination of the reader, a feature that explains much of the novel's popularity and success. I would like to point out, however, that anyone who has read only the American school edition of *Nothing* would believe the novel to be much more elliptical than it is in its full, original version. In that edition, twenty-eight passages have been left out, each averaging about two and one-half pages in the original Destino edition. Some of the interpretations discussed earlier would be incomprehensible without, for example, the passage recounting Don Jerónimo's confinement in the house on Aribau Street during the early days of the Civil War, or the passages dealing with Andrea's relationship with Gerardo, which precedes her relationship with Pons and is essential to the development of her sexual awareness, or her last trip to the shower after witnessing the slit throat of Román, underscoring the ritualistic aspect of her use of the shower in the novel. Save for this caveat, it is proper to recognize the value of the school text with its fine introduction, notes, and questions. *Nada* is immensely popular with college-age students, and it would be unfortunate to deprive them of this excellent and important novel, which might be too long or inaccessible in its full, original version.

CHAPTER 4

La isla y los demonios *(The Island and the Devils)*, La mujer nueva *(The New Woman)*, *and* La insolación *(Sunstroke)*

I *Introduction*

I T is convenient to treat Laforet's other three full-length novels as a group, both because they have a great deal in common and because much of what has been explored in *Nothing* applies to these works as well. The theme of self-fulfillment is central to the later novels as it was to the first, although approached from a unique perspective in each book. *La isla y los demonios* (The Island and the Devils) centers on a young Canary Island girl's dreams of becoming a writer; the time is the late 1930s, when the Civil War was raging on the mainland. *La mujer nueva* (The New Woman) treats a young woman's conversion to Catholicism and her struggle to reconcile her former life with her new life; a provincial Leonese town and Madrid are the geographical focal points for these two phases of her life. *La insolación* (Sunstroke), which examines the adolescence of a boy with talent for painting, takes place in three successive summers (1940–1942) on the Mediterranean coast. The art motif and spatial ambience are significant in these three works as they are in *Nothing*, but the technical handling is different. Laforet's techniques and store of wisdom about life advance in some respects in the later novels, but she never again achieves the startling fresh vision of *Nothing*, partly because she never again employs the complex first-person narrator. In this chapter I will outline the salient elements of each novel individually, and then conclude with an archetypal analysis of the underlying paradigm inherent in all four novels.

II   La isla y los demonios *(The Island and the Devils)*

The Island and the Devils, following in the wake of *Nothing*, although seven years later, naturally invites comparison with the first novel, which achieved such wide acclaim. There are several superficial similarities between the two works: (1) an isolated and alienated adolescent female protagonist, (2) a closed familial and spatial ambience from which she wishes to escape (though the family hatreds and struggles are slightly more muted in *The Island* than in *Nothing*), and (3) the Civil War as historical background. As in *Nothing*, the family in *The Island* is the center of the action, that is, a substitute family. Marta, like Andrea, is an orphan of sorts. Her father died in an automobile accident, plunging her mother, Teresa, into a catatonic state from which she never recovers. Marta lives on the family's country estate with her stepbrother José and his wife, Pino. (The mother is also on the premises, locked away in her room.) José apparently suffers insecurity at being only indirectly related to the family fortune (Marta is heir to her mother's estate, since José is only a stepson); he has become overly protective of the honor of the women in the family. He does not allow Pino to leave the estate alone, and he tries similarly to control Marta's life. But Marta, whose love of freedom is shared by all Laforet's heroines, manages to thwart José's attempts to restrain her.

Marta, like Andrea, embarks on a quest for freedom and self-discovery. But, whereas *Nothing* explored the awakening of adolescent self-awareness and sexuality through encounters with art with the theme of personal artistic formation only latent in the narrative, *The Island* concentrates directly on the awakening of the adolescent artistic imagination as a parallel to that of the sexual self. Marta, heiress to a respectable fortune, does not first have to stabilize her economic situation before she can allow her imaginary powers to develop. She is free to devote herself to the artistic side of life from the beginning, and perhaps her very isolation and idleness have fostered her artistic interests.

Marta has literary ambitions and is writing a series of "Legends of Alcorah" (a native Canary Island god, whose name probably derives from Arabic). These legends deal with folklore of the Canary

Island natives, a large race of people, possibly related to the Vikings. The beauty and mystery of the Islands and their lore are important leitmotifs in the book. Vicenta, the peasant servant, is a vehicle for some of this lore, which is interwoven with the other motifs: art, fantasy, and reality. The central theme, the juxtaposition of imagination and reality, grows admirably out of the setting with its incredible natural beauty, the enchantment of its ocean, mountains, and native folklore.

In *Nothing* the heroine embarked upon her journey to self-development by going to the city. The situation is reversed in *The Island*; Marta's "sophisticated" peninsular relatives take refuge on the island, escaping the holocaust of the Civil War on the mainland. Their arrival signals the beginning of Marta's maturation through a succession of encounters between her childish dreams and the reality of the world outside her fantasies. As in *Nothing* the heroine's development takes place in about a year (beginning in the fall of 1938 and ending in the late summer of 1939, after the victory of the Franco forces), and it is likewise divided into three parts. There is a major difference, however, in the narrative style of the two novels; the awakening is not told directly by Marta, but by an omniscient third person, although the point of view is essentially Marta's. An exception is found in the central portion of the third part, in which each of the other characters has a section to meditate upon his own hopes, frustrations, and shattered dreams, with the consequent shifting of narrative perspective.

Laforet seems to reverse Faulkner's technique of *The Sound and the Fury*, in which the story of a family is told by each of its members and then retold by an omniscient narrator in a final section. There are other similarities, aside from the revolving viewpoint, between this novel and Faulkner's: (1) family decadence viewed in the setting of the old family home, (2) a brother (Jason and José), whose pecuniary interests and concern for his promiscuous sister's virtue are constant sources of tension, even violence, and (3) a mother rendered useless by continual illness and confinement. It is entirely possible that Laforet had *The Sound and the Fury* and/or *As I Lay Dying* in mind when she wrote *The Island and the Devils;* she had just discussed Faulkner in her *Destino* column earlier in the year (see Chapter 2).

The first part of the novel, comprising six of the twenty chapters, focuses on the arrival of the mainland relatives to the island and establishes the central theme of fantasy and illusion versus reality, with its subordinate motifs: art, superstition, and disillusionment. The first scene portrays the arrival of Marta and José's relatives, Daniel, Honesta, and Matilde, accompanied by Pablo, a painter friend; all are refugees seeking asylum from the Civil War in the home of their well-to-do nephew. The opening, depicting their debarkation, sets the stage for the development of interpersonal tensions that ensue during their stay on the island. First, Marta is seen from several angles on the wharf, alone and then in relation to José and Pino:

Marta Camino moved as close as she could to the water on the wharf, where the mail boat from the Peninsula was to tie up. Her diminutive adolescent figure was outlined for a moment against the light, with her dark skirt and light, short-sleeved sweater. The breath of the sea was very light that day and gently lifted her short, shiny, straw-colored hair. She covered her eyes with her hand; her entire face seemed anxious and expectant. The boat, at that moment, was turning around the large breakwater and entered the Luz Harbor. (N, p. 351)

Marta's apparent solitude is abruptly curtailed by the voice of her stepbrother, bringing her back to reality: "—Are you crazy? You're making Pino nervous; she says you're going to fall.— He made her step back a few paces, and now the girl was between her brother and sister-in-law. In that position, between the two, she looked infantile and insignificant" (N, pp. 351–52). The perspective then shifts to the four mainland visitors, arriving with their own set of expectations. The paradigm is complete in the opening pages: Marta is a chrysalis, nearly ready to take flight, but there are several obstacles she must hurdle before she can emerge into a new, more mature stage of life: (1) awakening of feelings of sex and love, (2) the death of her mother, and (3) modification of her literary aspirations, after accepting a more realistic view of her talent.

In the first part, Marta matures little, but suffers a certain amount of disillusionment. The peninsular relatives (literally the symbols of the great world beyond the immediately confining family and environment) serve as the catalysts in Marta's maturation process. Marta has keenly looked forward to the arrival of her relatives because they, as artists themselves—Daniel is a mediocre composer and director, Matilde a sometime poetess—will surely be more interested in her own budding literary attempts than José or Pino. Part of Marta's initiation is a confrontation with and acceptance of the human limitations of these people. They are not the great artists she had imagined. They are not even particularly admirable people; Daniel is an effeminate hypochondriac and Matilde is humorless and self-centered.

In the second part (Chapters 7 through 14), Marta places her hopes on Pablo, the painter friend, with whom she becomes infatuated in a kind of first puppy love. The coordination of Marta's two lines of development, artistic and sexual, is effected in several ways through this relationship. Marta's encounters with Pablo begin when she finds a sketching pad she supposes to belong to Pablo. Her Aunt Honesta's indiscreetly open legs are drawn on one sheet; on another she sees a scratched-out figure of a hoofed devil, reminiscent of Picasso's drawings of satyrs, and some strange lines depicting a man beating a woman, resembling José and Pino.

Laforet introduces into this part the techniques of paintinglike descriptions she employed in *Nothing*; these are lacking in the first section of *The Island and the Devils*. When Marta goes to Pablo's room in Chapter 7 to return his sketching pad, his room is portrayed in a way that calls to mind Van Gogh's painting of his room at Arles:

The room was simple. A bed, a wardrobe, a coatrack, a basin with running water, practically filled it. Pablo had not added any imagination; there were not even any papers with drawings, nor painter's tools. Nothing of his, not even a cigarette butt in the ash tray... Only an overcoat hanging limply on the coatrack indicated that the room had not been abandoned altogether. . . . [The luminous, blue sea atmosphere enters through the one window.] (*N*, p. 447)

Marta and Pablo meet every day for conversation until Pablo ends the relationship, apparently out of embarrassment at having told Marta too much about his private life and perhaps because local tongues are beginning to wag. Without the company of Pablo, Marta falls into a relationship with a handsome young man with whom she swims and whom she is seen kissing on a remote beach. Again local gossip carries the story to José, who, enraged about family honor, confines Marta to her room for several weeks. At this point she decides to flee the island by stowing away on board the ship in which her relatives plan to sail to the mainland. By this time the war has ended, and Daniel, Matilde, Honesta, and Pablo are making preparations to return to Madrid.

Throughout the second part, Marta has gained an ever-increasing sense of reality; she displays a better-formed personality than in the first part. Laforet combines island lore with the self-awareness theme early in this part to mark the onset of the fundamental change:

Marta was leaning her head against the trunk of a *drago* tree. It is a tree of centuries, almost human. A tree whose twisted trunk suggests passionately entwined bodies; its crown of hard, sharp leaves, like little century plants, scratches the smoothness, the silk of the sky, and a red sap runs down its bark. It is not a good idea to think about the one you love with your head leaning against this tree of warm lands. Its silent mystery is not shrouded in mists; it is outlined sharply in the brilliant, chilless light. It demands reality. It refuses shadows; if the knife cuts it, it does not disguise its juices as freshness and water; it unleashes blood like a man's flesh when it is wounded. Centuries and centuries it remains quietly waiting beneath the sun and the warm nights of low stars.

Marta felt behind her head the palpitation of that bloody wisdom of the *drago* tree. "Reality, reality, kisses in the night, kisses... Reality, Marta Camino. What did you expect from this man, this friend? He won't give you anything. You don't love him. He will never give you children. He makes you dream the purity of life and of art. But, what is that? Life for a woman is love and reality. Love, reality, palpitation of the blood. Your wide mouth is sad and breathes voluptuousness, although your eyes are pure. You have in you the seeds of many children, who will be born; you are like a new savage land and you must wait like the earth, quietly, for the moment to bear plants." (*N*, p. 465)

Thus her final rejection of art (fantasy) as a viable mode of life is foreshadowed.

The end of the second part includes a trip to the south to visit Pablo, ostensibly to seek his advice about escaping the island. She remains infatuated with him until very near the end of the novel, when she overhears Pablo trying to make love to a reluctant Honesta on the night of Teresa's death. The final scene of the second part (like the first scene, also a visit to Pablo) again employs description that imitates painting; the landscape of the south is pictured in terms reminiscent of Cézanne's pre-Cubist renderings of French villages (cf. Chapter 2).

The third and final part (Chapters 15 through 20) signals Marta's freedom from the bondage of her familial home. Marta's mother has died suddenly, and José (probably out of self-interest) is now willing to let Marta go openly to Madrid with the relatives to study. Teresa, while locked away in her room, a mysterious shadow in the background of the novel, serves as a focal point either through personal interest or by providing a contrasting character for other personages. José, with a childhood infatuation for his stepmother, married Pino, Teresa's nurse, to keep Pino chained to Teresa's side. Pino, resentful of her servitude and restricted life, is accused by José of murdering Teresa. Marta, the legitimate daughter, seems to have no feeling for her mother at all. Vicenta, the stalwart native servant, remains in José's service only to protect Teresa, whom she believes to be the victim of an evil spell. Compared to Teresa's natural beauty and charm, some traces of which are still visible, Matilde is plain and unfeminine, Honesta vapid and vulgar.

Teresa's death is the motive for all the characters to converge on the country estate, and during the nightlong wake (again reminiscent of Faulkner) each character has an opportunity to let his mind drift over his past life. Matilde's memories reveal her as a young, talented woman, who has narrowed her life by marrying the pompous, chauvinistic Daniel. José's unpleasant, possessive personality is given psychological depth, when he reflects on the way his relatives treated him as a child; they considered him retarded. Teresa was the only member of the family to have faith in his ability and to consider him with respect and dignity. His father, Luis, a philanderer, paid little attention to him or to his gracious second wife. Every character has had his or her dreams and illusions, as has Marta; all have been scarred or broken by the undeniably harsh realities of life.

The principal theme of *The Island and the Devils*, imagination and fantasy, the heart of artistic creation, is a natural adjunct of the island setting. The island, with its unreal ambience, brilliant seascapes, volcanic irregularities, profuse and colorful vegetation, and openness of spirit manifest in the native folklore, legends, and songs, fosters the imagination. Too, the island suggests the distance necessary to creation. The backdrop of terrible events occurring on the mainland and the physical remoteness of the Canaries (Matilde is constantly repeating the refrain, "One would hardly know a war was going on") reminds us that spatial as well as temporal distances are important to art. *Nothing* relied upon the temporal dimension;

74   CARMEN LAFORET

in *The Island* geography is more important. There is a tacit suggestion that the peninsula is reality while the island is fantasy,
unreality.

The Island contains yet another symbolic dimension in the enclosure motif. Unfulfilled aspirations are related to incarceration as
Pino, and later Marta, are closed up in the country house by José,
and Teresa is literally imprisoned there. Matilde comments that she
has been "locked up on an island." The island becomes a place from
which to escape for Marta; she claims she will never return. Thus
a dialectic of closed/open, house/sea, island/peninsula imagery is
constructed to underscore hindrances to and means by which growth
may take place. Fantasy, when it serves to deny reality, is a kind
of personal enclosure. In the end Marta will have to leave the island,
symbol of her entrapment in a life of unreality.

The devils of the title have two references in the novel: the devils
of island folklore and the human passions that fuse with the island's
enchantment in the creation of art: "Art, according to Pablo, was
the only way to personal salvation. The only consolation in
life . . . . Art saves us from the inferno of this life. All the devils
in us become angels through art" (*N*, p. 455). Art can be "a devil
that pushes us" (*N*, p. 476). Laforet believes in retrospect that the
title of the novel is too long and that it lacks the impact of the
succinct *Nothing*. This may be true in a purely aesthetic sense, but
the title *The Island and the Devils* does capture the juxtaposition
of nature (geography) and the human passions that forms the basic
tension and meaning of the book.

Laforet summarizes the novel as "the dreams, the blindnesses,
the intuitions and rude awakenings [that] are a harsh reality in the
course of a few months in the life of an adolescent girl" (*N*, p. 347).
Actually all the characters have engaged in fantasy of some kind.
José dreams of financial independence, which will give him the
personal security he needs before starting a family and establishing
his own little patriarchal dynasty. Pino longs for the death of Teresa
and a freer, more congenial life in the city. The mainlanders represent mostly shipwrecked dreams: Matilde has given up writing
to dedicate herself to the war effort and places her hopes for artistic
creation in her talentless, spineless husband, Daniel. Daniel, rather
than fulfilling his promise to write great symphonies, has become
a sad bundle of ulcers and nervous tics. Honesta simply looks ridiculous in her attempts to be the understanding woman, giving

comfort to the "great" artist Pablo, who in turn proves to have his own collection of failed aspirations and dashed hopes. Teresa assumes the extreme attitude of complete immobility, when her desire for a happy life with José's father is crushed. Vicenta, as the only true product of the island, is the single character for whom the reality/fantasy dichotomy does not exist. Within her the two are completely fused; her dreams are reality (she dreams of an impending catastrophe before Teresa's death and has a strange presentiment before her daughter is knifed for provoking her jealous boyfriend). When Teresa dies she melds back into her native region, never to be seen again.

Marta's fantasies encompass nearly every aspect of her life: the island, escape, her writing, her relatives, love. The process of disillusionment is gradual; she prolongs her dreams even when reality has already begun to deny them. She knowingly lies to her friends about her "artistic" relatives (the "magical beings" *N*, p. 358), pretending that Matilde is very interested in her "Legends of Alcorah" and that Daniel has nearly completed a symphony of the Canary Islands. Marta is often seen fantasizing and daydreaming while others are engaged in banal day-to-day living; other characters repeatedly startle her from her reveries. Her final, seemingly definitive emergence from her dream-world and girlish illusions culminates with the burning of the "Legends of Alcorah," symbol of girlhood self-centeredness and the remoteness from reality of the islands and their lore. She has the good sense or good fortune to recognize the pitfalls of fantasy and counter them with action, before she becomes embittered by disillusionment, as have most of the adults who surround her.

Art has a different function in *The Island and the Devils* than it does in *Nothing*; the creative imagination is the theme rather than the method of the second novel. In *The Island*, because of its third-person perspective, there is no assurance that Marta will ever write again, whereas in *Nothing* Andrea's artistic endeavor is latently implicit in the narrative irony. There is, however, another kind of narrative irony in *The Island and the Devils* that points the way to Marta's probable future as a nonwriter. Her development has reflected that of the adults in her life—namely, gradual disenchantment: "[Marta] would never return to being the blind, happy creature of before, after having been bitten by the devils" (*N*, p. 624). She understands many more things about life and art now; her

awakening rather than to art (as with Andrea) was an awakening to
reality: "Marta well knew that Pablo was not such a great artist that
he would give up his wife for painting, even though it might be the
case that he could not do both things at once: love her and create
his art" (N, p. 628). By analogy one is led to conclude that Marta's
life on the mainland will continue to divorce her from the imaginary.

Joaquín de Entrambasaguas[1] believes that the major part of *The
Island and the Devils* was written before *Nothing,* a conjecture
probably based largely on Laforet's own biography; the girl in *The
Island* is younger (sixteen instead of eighteen) and the action takes
place in Laforet's childhood home. But *The Island* was written in
its entirety long after *Nothing* and is more related in tone and spirit
to Laforet's life in the late 1940s and early 1950s than to her childhood. While she was writing *The Island and the Devils,* she made
her only return trip to the Canaries (1951); she wrote several travel
articles about the trip as well, expressing the feeling of freedom and
enchantment that the islands hold for her.[2] Another article written
earlier in the same year, "Leyendo 'El camino,' " concerning a novel
by Miguel Delibes, perhaps gives a clue to the source of the name
Camino (road) she assigns to Marta's family. Like Delibes's main
character in *El camino,* Marta learns to cope with growing up and
the unpleasant realities of adult life.

Laforet says that in *The Island and the Devils* she fulfilled a
longtime desire to express "the special, luminous enchantment that
I saw in my adolescence in the land of the Great Canary Island. A
dry land, with harsh crags and gentle nooks full of flowers and huge
canyons always battered by the wind" (N, p. 347). As with *Nothing*
her expressed intent was to capture the feeling for a place, which
she does admirably, but again, as in *Nothing,* the real achievement
is the uncannily vivid exploration of an artistic adolescent's consciousness as it awakens to its surroundings, not only physical but
psychological and social as well.

III   La mujer nueva (*The New Woman*)

La mujer nueva (The New Woman) seems to constitute a radical
shift in Laforet's novelistic material heretofore. Rather than an adolescent, the protagonist, Paulina (after St. Paul), is an adult, married woman, who "converts" to Catholicism after a mystic experience.
But the fundamental pattern of the third novel is the same as that

of the first two; Paulina's experience, like those of Andrea and Marta, is a groping for self-identity and fulfillment, with the difference that Paulina's struggle centers on or within her conscience rather than on her environment. This is not to say that environment is unimportant in *The New Woman*, but that it is important in a different way. Rather than an antagonist, the environment is included in its role as a psychological determinant. In the interval between the writing of *The Island and the Devils* and *The New Woman*, Carmen Laforet appears to have added depth psychology to her reading list and thus to her novelistic canon. Not only is Paulina's conversion handled with great complexity as a psychological, social, and moral problem, but some of the characters actually quote Freud and Adler in referring to Paulina's seemingly unbalanced personality.

The theme of *The New Woman* is the struggle for the conscience to mature when confronted with those moral aspects of life which form an integral part of accepting adult responsibilities. The moral choices Paulina faces do not even exist for girls the age of Marta and Andrea. To achieve the social aspect of this struggle, the narrative viewpoint is wholly omniscient. The narrator shifts focus from one character to another to highlight his or her relationship to Paulina. While this narrative technique is appropriate to the purposes of *The New Woman*, it is less interesting and less innovative than those used in either of the first two novels. *The New Woman*, like its predecessors, is divided into three parts, but the triptych arrangement here is designed to set off and frame the conversion experience that occurs in the central portion. The first part is a study from various points of view of Paulina's life and personality up to the time of her conversion; the third part, of equal or slightly greater length, deals with her life as a convert and her efforts to accommodate her new life to her responsibilities as wife and mother. The second part, the conversion, is brief and intense.

In the first section we learn of Paulina's alienation from her parents, whom she thought hypocritical; her father, a mining engineer, was a political conservative and therefore supported the Church, but he blasphemed and had mistresses, flaunting the Church's values. Paulina's jealous mother spent her days in church seeking solace for her pride, wounded by a philandering husband; the priests offered her no consolation, telling her she must be strong and endure. When Paulina goes to the university in Madrid, where she lives with a kindly grandmother, she naturally falls in with free-

thinking friends, who talk openly about the hypocrisy of Church
morality. After finishing her university degree (June 1936), she
meets Eulogio on the train back to their provincial village in León.
Eulogio has long been Paulina's neighbor, but she did not really
know him, because they are from different social strata: Eulogio
belongs to the old, landed gentry of liberal political persuasion, and
Paulina's father represents the new technocrats of conservative
orientation. They fall in love just before the outbreak of the Spanish
Civil War (July 18, 1936). Paulina's father is killed by leftists; Eulogio's father (a leftist) succumbs later in the war. In the free-think-
ing spirit of leftists at the time, Paulina and Eulogio consider
themselves united without benefit of clergy and go to Barcelona
together to participate in the Revolution underway there.

When Paulina becomes pregnant they submit to a civil marriage.
This point will later serve as a possible escape from the marriage
for Paulina (civil marriages were not recognized in Spain under
Franco) and will make her struggle to decide whether or not to
remain in the marriage a legitimate problem. Divorce was not allowed in post–Civil War Spain. When Franco's Nationalist forces
finally gain control of the entire country, Paulina is seven months'
pregnant, and Eulogio leaves her behind to help his Republican-
sympathizing relatives escape to France. Finding it too dangerous
to return to Spain, Eulogio embarks for Central America, whence
he writes his relatives to look after Paulina. Eulogio's cousin Antonio
finds her in prison, where she has given birth to her child. Antonio
and his wealthy, influential father arrange for her release, and Antonio, eight years younger than Paulina, becomes infatuated with
the gaunt, dark-eyed woman, whom he finds different from all other
women he knows. Even though she is not pretty, Paulina has always
fascinated men. She had no girlfriends at the university, because
the other girls feared she would attract away their boyfriends. Paulina accepts Antonio's friendship but rejects his amorous advances.
Discouraged, he finally marries into a moneyless but titled family
in Villa de Robre, the Leonese town where Eulogio and Paulina
grew up.

The novel opens with Paulina on the way to the train station; she
is leaving Villa de Robre for some unexplained reason. The background to this scene is given gradually in a series of flashbacks.
Eulogio had returned from Central America a year and a half earlier;
unknown to Paulina he had become involved with a wealthy woman

there and had stayed abroad longer than political exigency would have required. When he returned, his attitude toward Paulina was changed; the total love and commitment to each other they had shared during the war had vanished. Paulina became pregnant again, and Mariana, Eulogio's strong, organization-minded mother, insisted that they move from Madrid to León so that she could care for delicate Paulina. Paulina suffered a miscarriage and a long illness in Villa de Robre. Upon recovering, she succumbed to the adulterous love offered by Antonio, now living in the village with his wife's family. But after two months of the affair, Paulina's conscience overcame her (partly because Antonio's wife has a terminal illness), and she decided to escape to Madrid. So ends the first part.

The second part, the conversion, takes place on the train at the moment when Paulina awakes in her sleeping compartment the next morning and gazes out at the flat, dry Castilian plain, the home of the great Spanish mystic poets Saint Teresa and Saint John of the Cross. In the few minutes she watches out the train window, she passes through the stages preparatory to an intense mystical experience. The Spanish mystics of the sixteenth century describe three general states: preparation, illumination, and finally union. The preparation requires quieting bodily sensation in order that the soul be free to emerge; in the second stage the soul sallies forth in search of the Divine partner:

[Paulina] now thought of nothing. Her head, her body, all her senses were serene at this pure moment of waking. . . . The mountains of León had remained far away. Far, life... all that arduous, vulgar, little intrigue that was life. Far, the pain of body and soul... Everything far, except the immensities of earth and sky, high and pure. . . . This strange idea came to her like a deep desire for peace. . . . Because, like a tide, in small, slow waves, peace invaded her spirit. It was a divine sensation. . . . She saw a reddish glow, more spectacular by the minute, wide and powerful, surrounded by small, golden clouds, like flames on the horizon... (*N*, pp. 1130–32)

She writes Blanca (Antonio's beatific mother-in-law), who has been cultivating Paulina's spiritual side during and since her long illness. The conversion is not as sudden and psychologically unmotivated as it might appear. Blanca has been successful in her spiritual tutelage of Paulina, because she is a sad, lonely, disillu-

sioned woman, whose every attempt to find love has been thwarted
or embittered. Her mystic experience on the train ends with her
feeling

mysteriously united to the men and women of the entire world, with their
capacity for harm and destruction and also that other capacity, that other
thirst, that other search that is lost sometimes... The search for love. She
saw how she herself and everyone, even those that deny it, as a crime,
look for love. They look for it at times with the mentality of beasts and at
times with pain and blindness, and at times with a hatred of its traces and
its name... (N, p. 1132)

Paulina's story, like those of Marta and Andrea, is a quest; hers is
a quest for love, which she finally finds in a spiritual rather than a
carnal sense. Blanca puts Paulina in touch with a spiritual advisor
in Madrid, and she begins her spiritual cleansing and instruction.
   The long third part centers on Paulina's life alone in Madrid as
she wavers among her roles as wife, mother, mistress of Antonio,
and religious convert. This final section contains a story within a
story, which seems only peripherally related to Paulina's struggles
of conscience. It involves Amalia, Paulina's landlady of earlier times,
and her lazy, high-living son, Julián. Amalia, who has social pretensions above her station, has found it necessary to put the reluctant Julián to work. Paulina was instrumental in Julián's securing
a job with a maker of religious artifacts, living in her building. Julián
despises the manual labor he must perform and plots to rob the
shop-owner and his wife of some jewels he believes they will have
in their house on a particular day. Julián formulates an elaborate
plan that includes hiding in Paulina's apartment while she is away.
The plan miscarries, and in desperation Julián murders the woman
he had intended only to rob. Ironically Paulina's absence, which
makes Julián's plan feasible, is due to a trip with Antonio, a backsliding in her spiritual program. This subplot might seem to have
little bearing on the main subject of Paulina's conversion, but it
relates thematically to Paulina's final decision to return to her marriage and her child, by setting up a contrast between the murky
morality that exists in actual practice and the superficial purity of
religious theory.
   A meeting between Paulina and Julián in the street as Paulina
is returning from a religious retreat is presented twice, from the

contrasting viewpoints of each person. Julián has just been questioning the concierge of Paulina's building about Paulina's comings and goings, as part of the preparation of his criminal plan:

When he arrived at the corner, he had another unpleasant surprise. He saw Paulina. There was no doubt. He recognized her easily; they had lived in the same building so many years. And besides she was good-looking again, young. She was walking along on the sunny side of the street in a straw-colored jacket, with a small bag in hand, as if she were coming from a short trip. She had a smiling, introspective expression.

—Julián—she said kindly, almost happily, upon seeing him. —How are you?

Julián smiled with his best smile. He knew how to cover up and lose gracefully.

—Are you coming from work? Yes? I'm so glad! One of these days I'll go visit your mother.

Julián shot her a dirty word, undetectibly under his breath. He continued smiling, as she moved away. Then he remembered that he had not asked if she planned to remain in Madrid all summer. (*N*, pp. 1172–73)

The same scene is repeated a chapter later from Paulina's point of view. An ironic contrast is established between this repetition and the first telling of the encounter; Paulina has just left the convent, full of innocent, self-centered, spiritual thoughts, which seem rather ridiculous in the light of Julián's dark, desperate, evil cunning:

She was steeped in this desire [to open the world's eyes to the glories of religion and the Church], when she came out of the Metro station toward her apartment building, and she suddenly ran into Julián. Julián's smile was a smile of stupid, impressive sufficiency. Paulina felt a shock on seeing it. And as a reaction, the disagreeable sense of her own frivolity when she had been speaking to the priest. . . . (*N*, p. 1183)

After the gruesome murder, trial, and sentencing to death of Julián, Paulina reflects that Julián's greed is comparable to her own selfish search for momentary pleasures with Antonio or her self-centered denial of her son to pursue a religious vocation: "And before God, perhaps she, Paulina, was more guilty than that imbecile boy murderer" (*N*, p. 1260). The degree of guilt to be assigned a person's actions seems contingent upon the behavior expected of that person's maturity and level of moral awareness.

The end of the third part of the novel presents a series of choices to Paulina which must be considered in her efforts to achieve love and happiness. She wishes to take vows as a nun, but her confessor discourages that plan, urging her to return to Eulogio and Miguel, her son. Paulina herself postpones this desire when Miguel accuses her of not loving him and of thinking only about her religious vocation. In her only display of motherly tenderness in the entire novel, she promises Miguel she will not retire to a convent until he is older. Then she is tempted to marry Antonio, who is finally widowed, but she rejects this alternative as well. She ultimately decides to return to live with Eulogio, although it means living in an isolated village and even (for parts of the year) in the wilderness where Eulogio has his business. In making the decision, she believes that she is best serving the religious morality she has embraced as a convert, and her sacrifices in making the decision are multiple: she forgoes the possibility of a love-filled marriage with Antonio and the city life she prefers.

As Laforet has constructed the novel, Paulina's choices are absolutely incumbent upon her conscience: (1) she is free to remain with Eulogio or leave (Eulogio discovers that not even the civil marriage was recorded—for legal purposes, they were never married), and Eulogio is willing to accept her decision; (2) at first Antonio is not free legally, but it is evident from the outset that he eventually will be; (3) with enough display of dedication and years of prayer and isolation, Paulina's confessor would doubtless recommend her for a convent; and (4) Paulina has a university degree and teaching experience so that she could always maintain a separate existence of her own. Oddly enough, the last choice is the one she never really considers, perhaps because it was not a viable solution for a Spanish woman in the 1950s. Paulina's periods of independence are seen either as a transition—the nine-year wait for Eulogio's return— or as a decision-making time—her stay in Madrid after her conversion. In this sense the book is profoundly pessimistic; none of the other choices can be very rewarding. But the novel is not finally pessimistic, because Paulina believes that any life she chooses will be more fulfilling now that she has faith.

Of all Laforet's works, *The New Woman* contains the most explicit social criticism. It is a plea for a humanized Catholic Church, one that allows the consolation of faith without the attendant, destructive hypocrisy. *The New Woman* is in many ways a period piece, doc-

umenting the second decade of Franco's regime in Spain. The religious atmosphere dominated more than it had perhaps at any other
time in Spanish history since the era of Phillip II (1556–1598). By
the 1950s the Church had fully recovered from the losses suffered
under the Republic (the Constitution had severely limited the powers of the Church and clergy in public and private life). This ambience is reflected in Antonio, who "belonged to a new university
generation in Spain, which began in the National Movement. It was
a youth in which religious sentiment predominated in a large percentage" (*N*, p. 1267).

But this religious sentiment is not always very deep. For example,
Paulina has some friends, a couple who led a very interesting bohemian life in the early years after the war. Since Paulina was
alone—Eulogio was in Central America at the time—she frequently
joined these people for parties and literary discussions. She gave
up these contacts when Eulogio returned, but renews the friendships during her estrangement from Eulogio in Madrid. In the
interim, the couple has changed; they have taken on bourgeois
values and a pseudoreligiosity. Unaware of Paulina's recent spiritual
crisis, they talk lightheartedly of their attitude toward religion and
the Church:

—You talk like a Puritan, my dear, but really it would do you good to learn
some things about Catholicism. I tell you there has never been the kind
of piety there is now, and I tell you too that Rafael and I are convinced
that it is completely unsocial not to be a part of the Church. I won't say
that we have converted. That would be silly since we were baptized at
birth, but we practice our Catholicism publicly, like most of our friends...
There is none of this paganism you speak of; what has happened is that no
diversion nor any manner of living is contrary to piety. You have strange
ideas about this... If you think a bit you will get rid of all your fears about
practicing religion... (*N*, p. 1186)

After the Civil War such lay organizations as the Opus Dei and
Acción Católica were gaining strength and popularity. Paulina rejects joining Acción Católica, suggested by her advisor as a way to
fulfill her religious convictions:

Father, I don't think that is very effective, at least not here in Spain. Not
the way it is carried out. You tell me that Acción Católica is a group of lay
people who live normally, displaying Christ in their lives, in their kindly

way of treating people, in their generosity toward others, in their walks, in their work, in their dances... Demonstrating with their example and their smile what it is to love Christ. But the reality is, at least in Villa de Robre, which is where I have been able to observe the phenomenon, that none of this takes place. The pure souls (at least the women) are pointed to right away as half nuns. They dress in a strange way. They are prohibited from doing any number of healthy and perfectly legitimate things. It's just converted into another religious congregation, with the pretension—and this is the bad part—that they are lay people. They give the impression that when someone joins the Church, he is already a bit odd. (N, p. 1221)

The Church is also indirectly criticized for its policies on birth control; a woman in Paulina's neighborhood in Madrid continues to have children year after year even though her husband's salary cannot support them, and her own health is in jeopardy.

Even though the general tendency of the Spanish novel of the 1950s was to analyze Spanish social problems in a "realistic" narrative mode, no scholarly analysis of the implicit sociocritical aspect of Carmen Laforet's writing during this period has been undertaken. Nearly all criticism of *The New Woman* has been by ordained clerics, who approach the novel from a position of orthodoxy; they examine its fidelity to the psychology of a mystic experience and a religious conversion. The commentators are doubtless familiar with such cases via the confessions they hear. While these critics praise Laforet for writing a novel professing religious faith, they feel that Paulina's indecisiveness and backsliding, once the conversion has taken place, do not accurately reflect the convert's experience. Of course, from the purely literary point of view, Paulina's struggle is precisely what makes *The New Woman* an interesting novel.

The novel also derives strength and depth by using Paulina's religious crisis as a nucleus for a series of concerns related to religion and morality: (1) the Church's role in individual lives and society, (2) a woman's difficulties in finding love, happiness, and an appropriate place for herself in society, and (3) the development of adult moral responsibility. The core of each motif is contained in Carmen Laforet's greatly enriched handling of human psychology. Space in *The New Woman* is primarily interior space, through which a character moves and grows by means of encounters with good and evil.

IV   La insolación (*Sunstroke*)

The fourth novel returns to the adolescent world of *Nothing* and *The Island and the Devils,* but this time from a masculine point of view. The young protagonist, Martín, is a boy, although, like Andrea and Marta, he has a certain androgynous character in the beginning. Martín has other characteristics in common with Andrea: he is an orphan (of mother only) who lives part of the year with grandparents; he is an observer rather than an actor; his squalid life with his own family is changed and broadened, if less permanently than in Andrea's case, by contact with a more liberal and affluent family, the Corsis. Rather than portraying one entire year in Martín's life, Laforet, in three parts, develops Martín's growth and change during the three summers (1940, 1941, and 1942) spent with his father, Eugenio, and his stepmother, Adela, in the resort town of Beniteca. Though there is constant reference to the hunger and deprivation Spain was suffering during those years, in general, the war's aftermath is much less present than in *Nothing*. The violence and pent-up hostilities of *Nothing* have been supplanted by *machismo* and sibling relations based on masculinity and femininity as motivating forces. *La insolación* (Sunstroke) narrows its focus and concentrates on the struggle to achieve adulthood in a society of conflicting values, some provincial and traditional, others hedonistic and frivolous, whereas the personal and social aims of *Nothing* are diffuse.

In Part I, Martín, who is fifteen but still wears the short pants of a child, goes to Beniteca to visit his father for the first time since the father's remarriage. Martín's mother has been dead for some time, and since then he has lived with his maternal grandparents. Adela, the stepmother, resents the presence of her stepson, a resentment often countered by the swearing, supermasculine military man, Eugenio. Eugenio is overtly anxious that his son be extremely masculine like himself and so allows him much freedom of movement. Martín thus spends most of his time with two bizarre neighbors, Carlos (his own age) and Carlos's sister Anita (a year older). The Corsi children are motherless like Martín, but they present a contrast to his strict, traditional upbringing; having been raised in a free, adventuresome atmosphere, they are spoiled and mischievous. Their father, who appears only at the beginning and ending of the summers to collect the children, is involved in some mysterious, lucrative business, probably black-market dealings, common in those postwar years.

Corsi met the children's mother in a circus in the United States while still married to a wealthy American woman. He finally divorced the American woman and remarried when Carlos was about to be born. All this past family history is told by Frufru, the children's governess, originally hired away from the same circus to look after the American woman's children. Frufru is always described as quite old, but she has an ageless amount of energy and love of laughter and diversion. She lends a party and circus air to the estate rented by Corsi for his children's summer vacations. Frufru dyes her hair wild colors, wears heavy makeup, sequined dresses, and a flashy collection of costume jewelry.

The Corsi children's life of ease, play, and adventure counterpoints the general mood of terror and hunger in a Spain of which Martín's life is considerably more representative. The Corsis are always play-acting and joking; they never talk seriously about anything. They even incorporate Martín into their lives in a fictitious, dramatized manner, calling him *martín pescador* (kingfisher), partly because his Christian name suggests it and partly for his appearance. The kingfisher is a topheavy bird with a large beak and an unruly-looking shock of feathers atop its head. Martín is at an awkward stage of development, gawky, not filled out and well formed like his friend Carlos. The Corsis' use of a nickname for their friend sets him apart. Carlos and Anita are an inseparable unit as brother and sister; Martín is their sidekick. He accompanies them on their daily swim, watches them do recitations, and is generally available in a passive manner for the Corsi-planned activities. Martín does not initiate; he always follows.

Part I, the summer of 1940, introduces all the key elements of the novel: adolescents in a summer-vacation atmosphere, playing and exploring with very little consciousness of the greater world beyond (deprived post–Civil War Spain or the progress of World War II). There are short "interludes" of several pages between Parts I and II and Parts II and III which summarize Martín's winters with his grandparents in Alicante against the backdrop of current historical events. In the first interlude (the winter of 1940–1941) hunger is prevalent; there is no meat at all. A rapidly growing Martín must beguile his gaunt body with fried fish and almonds, the only sources of protein. Martín's grandmother recognizes his talent for painting and sacrifices certain household necessities to give him art lessons. Though Martín finds it difficult to concentrate on his regular school work, due to malnutrition and growing pains, he finds he can immerse himself in art. And he is at the threshhold of sexual awakening; he and the other boys at school have become interested in girls, but only to the point of talking and writing obscenities on bathroom walls.

Part II, the second summer, develops the dichotomy between the mature sexes only suggested in Part I. Anita shows the most change; she is now seventeen and the boys are sixteen. Anita contrives to be alone much of the time, escaping from the inseparable relationship she had with her brother the summer before. She talks of having lovers, flirts with soldiers, and generally acts in a promiscuous way that infuriates her brother. The boys have changed physically; they are taller and have a fuzzy suggestion of a beard, but their interests still tend more to childish roughhousing. Adela, who gave birth to a daughter the previous February, is constantly preoccupied with Eugenio's seeming preference for Martín, the male child. Pregnant again, Adela claims that Martín's presence makes her ill. These prejudices and animosities crystallize in the culminating event toward the end of the novel. As in *Nothing* there is no real plot, but rather a series of events that have ritualistic significance in terms of adolescent growth and maturity. And, as in *Nothing*, Laforet includes a pivotal incident that lends mystery, intrigue, and tension to the novel. In *Nothing* this incident is Ena's affair with Román, her rejection of him, and his suicide.

In *Sunstroke* the incident centers on Eugenio's preoccupation with his son's masculinity. The animosity of several other characters toward Martín finds an easy instrument against the boy in the father's extremely rigid values. Part II sets the stage for the festering of these animosities, including the hatred of Don Clemente, the village doctor, for Martín. This hatred, which will eventually cause the central crisis, is somewhat complexly introduced. Carlos Corsi believes he has heard voices in the atticlike room contained in a little tower on their summer house; the room is immediately above Carlos's bedroom. Everyone else is sure that he hears rats. One day, when Anita has skipped off to have a tryst with the doctor's son in town, Carlos is determined to find his sister. He is convinced that she is hiding in the attic, because he has just heard the voices again. Carlos and Martín climb on the roof to enter the attic as the housekeeper claims the key has been lost. While the two are climbing on the roof and shortly before Carlos falls and breaks his arm, Martín has an intuition that Anita is with the doctor's son. Martín reveals this to Carlos while the Corsi boy writhes in pain on the ground, but he overcomes the pain in order to pursue Anita in town.

Carlos faints at the door of the doctor's house as he screams for his sister to come out. Anita finally does emerge and immediately becomes engaged in an argument with the doctor's wife, who accuses Anita of trying to compromise her son's virtue. In the midst of the fray, the doctor tries to attend to Carlos, over Anita's protests. She does not want her brother attended by a doctor in whose house she is not welcome. Finally they take Carlos home without setting his arm, but Don Clemente does come several days later to set it. Of course, this belated treatment is extremely painful, and Carlos and Anita believe Don Clemente has purposely made the setting as painful as possible out of spite. Several days later Eugenio's dog is killed with glass in its food; it is the second time in a year that someone has killed a dog belonging to Eugenio by this method. The children, who were quite fond of the dog, suspect Don Clemente, the doctor, and decide to take revenge on him.

Don Clemente has shown a middle-aged man's interest in the flirtatious Anita, so Carlos and Martín set a trap for the doctor into which Anita coquettishly leads him, with the result that the boys brutally beat the doctor one night in the woods. For the time being Don Clemente, in order not to reveal his lascivious leanings, merely says he has fallen down during his nightly rounds. The beating is witnessed by a mysterious presence, a person with a hunting knife, hiding stealthily in a tree. The only reference to this mysterious presence in the first part of the novel is a feeling Martín has sometimes at night in his room of being under surveillance. The mysterious presence and the noises Carlos has heard upstairs are solved at the end of Part II, when Damián, the housekeeper's husband, a Republican Civil War refugee, is discovered hiding in the attic. Damián represents a moment of historical reality in the vacation atmosphere of the three long parts of the novel. When the Civil War ended in 1939, many Republicans were trapped within Spain with no means of escape to take refuge outside the country. In the first months after the war, the Franco regime jailed and often shot those who had participated actively on the Republican side. This situation forced many trapped Republicans to become "internal exiles," hunted animals within their own country, living, like Damián, in seclusion with the aid of relatives. Their families pretended they had died in the conflict; some refugees existed in this fashion, hiding in interior rooms of the house or in woods or caves for scores of years. The last emerged in 1977.

The second interlude (winter of 1940–1941) emphasizes Martín's progress with his art and briefly mentions the World War raging beyond the borders of a beleaguered Spain that remains nominally neutral in order to recover from her own recent holocaust. The schoolboys are now actively seeking the company of girls, but Martín finds walking around with and talking frivolously to girls very boring. The topic of a woman's role in society is brought up by Martín in conversation with his grandmother. He wonders if women are capable of higher learning. His grandmother answers that women should remain in the home, looking after their husbands and children. Martín's own mother finished a degree, but then, at age thirty, she married Eugenio, a military man, inferior to her in the grandmother's opinion. Her studies had served her for nothing. This topic leads into the news that Adela has had another girl child, and the grandfather comments that Adela seems capable only of producing female offspring.

In Part III (summer of 1942), the theme of adolescent androgyny transforming into specific sexuality explodes in several dangerous directions. Anita, now eighteen, does not arrive in Beniteca with Carlos. She is touring with her father and a wealthy Latin American who writes bad poetry and clearly dotes on Anita. Typically she plays the coquette with him, further alienating and infuriating Carlos. In Anita's absence, Carlos and Martín develop a game they call lizard-hunting, flirting with girls their own age on the beach. During the San Juan festival the two boys are seen at the fair, arm in arm. Malicious gossip (probably initiated by the still-seething Don Clemente) insinuates a homosexual relationship between the boys. Eugenio forbids Martín to attend the fair the following night with Carlos and Frufru, but Martín slips out the window to accompany his friends against his father's wishes. Eugenio punishes Martín, but not too severely; he is clearly not too concerned about disobedience, only unmasculine behavior.

When Anita arrives a few weeks later, Carlos immediately gives up his diversions with Martín and attempts to reestablish the threesome of the past two summers. Martín is disappointed that Carlos so easily gives up the camaraderie that had sprung up between them in Anita's absence, but he acquiesces to Carlos's preferences. Anita, now definitely uninterested in the childish activities of Carlos and Martín, prefers to spend her time in more sophisticated automobile excursions and outings with the wealthy Latin American, who has stayed on in Beniteca out of infatuation with Anita.

Carlos, ever more frustrated with his sister's independence, decides to make her jealous by pretending to spend the night at the local brothel, but is too cowardly to carry out the threat and sneaks into Martín's room instead. This will just as effectively serve the purpose of allowing him to arrive home at dawn and appear to have had a night of carousing. The plan works, and Anita begins to pay more attention to him, so he uses the ruse a second night. This time Adela sees Carlos cross the yard and climb up to Martín's room. The situation perfectly suits her wish to remove her hated stepson from the house. She wakes Eugenio, who, upon finding his son and Carlos in bed together, beats Martín and locks him in his room while considering having him sent to a correctional institution. Adela, pretending to help Martín and perhaps feeling genuinely sorry she has thus damaged the boy's life, urges him to escape and return to his grandparents in Alicante. At first Martín refuses, hoping to convince his father of his innocence. But when he learns that Carlos, who escaped when Eugenio entered his bedroom, has gone off on an excursion with the Latin American and Anita for the day, as though nothing had happened, Martín in excruciating loneliness and rage succumbs to Adela's pleading and leaves for Alicante. There, his grandmother welcomes the beaten, bruised Martín back warmly and without questions.

The last fifty pages bring into focus the underlying currents of the novel. Parallel to the adolescent ritual of maturation is the theme of the serious, artistically oriented spirit confronted with a world of deprivation and narrow-mindedness on the one hand (Adela and Eugenio) and thoughtless, amoral frivolity on the other (the Corsis). At one point Martín realizes that his art is much more important to him than anything else, especially more important than what he had thought to be his all-important friendship with Carlos. In a dialogue-at-cross-purposes, while Carlos talks about his sister, Martín tries to explain to his friend how he feels about painting:

—Yesterday, I realized what it means to have the vocation of artist, Carlos. Stay here a moment. I beg you to listen to me for once. I think you and I can talk like intelligent people for a minute. Yesterday during those hours in which I was thinking, I felt what true liberation is. I don't know if you have ever confronted the problems of religious, political, and family ties. I don't know. We've never talked. I felt liberated from all that, as if I had broken the ropes.[3]

Martín's attempt to initiate a deeper conversation with Carlos is futile; the Corsi boy's thoughts remain on his sister. Martín has clearly matured, if not sexually, at least socially and spiritually. He is forming a mind and vocation of his own, independent of the values of his parents and society, thinking for himself. Ironically, later in the same afternoon, Carlos calls Martín a fanatical Spaniard, who "believes in everything or believes in nothing, [who] can't be tolerant like us [the Corsis]" (p. 330). The Corsis are tolerant precisely because they have no roots, no beliefs, no ties to family or society. Their father is an economic parasite, a black-market dealer; they have lived in numerous places but owe allegiance to none. Their credo is to live well however they can, at the expense of whomever is willing to be used (Mr. Corsi has borrowed a great deal of money from the Latin American, for example, and seems to be using his daughter for collateral). The Corsis, at least the children, talk and think of nothing more than play-acting and diversion. They live a glittering, showy, circus life amidst the pathos and hunger surrounding them. The name Corsi suggests several things: (1) the word *cursi* in Spanish, which means insubstantial in quality, and (2) the word for running, moving, in Italian. The Corsis are itinerant and without values; they have no means of understanding or appreciating the depths to which life reaches in history or art. Damián's story reminds the reader of the other side of life, as do the references to hunger and World War II in the interludes.

When Martín attempts to explain to the superficial Carlos what his art means to him—"To be able to do without everything is to have the strength and the basis to create" (p. 327)—Carlos proclaims that his friend has suffered a sunstroke. And Martín realizes that this is true, albeit not in the literal, physical sense that Carlos means it, but rather in a figurative, spiritual sense:

In truth, the entire summer in Beniteca—the three summers united in a long, flaming summer—constituted a huge sunstroke, not in the sense in which Carlos had spoken, but on the contrary. Not because Martín had become enthusiastic about his art, but because he forgot it. He forgot everything in Beniteca. (p. 329)

Martín's artistic imagination is beginning to take shape. In his final conversation with Carlos, he uses a phrase in Latin meaning "a woman whose beautiful breast terminates in a hideous fish." On the same day, he draws for the Corsis for the first time, imitating Picasso's style in a picture of a harlequin. Anita thinks the drawing is terrible. The people in *Sunstroke*, like Picasso's harlequins of

92 CARMEN LAFORET

1915, reflect a sad circus world; the characters whose role it is to
make people laugh are sidelined and depicted in their ironic tragedy
in a beach setting. Carlos and Anita are useless jesters; the only
difference between them and Picasso's harlequins is that they are
unaware of their own futility. Carlos interrupts Anita and Martín's
discussion of Picasso's merits: "Well, let's stop wasting time, O.K.?
We've always had fun together, and I don't know what's happened
this year that we don't seem able to have a good time" (p. 328).
The parallel between Picasso's harlequins and Laforet's characters
is appropriate, too, because Picasso painted his figures during the
First World War and Martín imitates them during the Second World
War.

When Martín thinks of returning to his grandmother's house in
Alicante after the violent misunderstanding with his father, he
thinks in pictorial terms; his art will doubtless be his salvation from
the superficiality of the Corsis and the narrow-mindedness of his
father: "The idea of his room with the desk and the little window
next to the ceiling where at night the light from the patio streamed
in and reflected on the wall across in superimposed squares, as in
a painting, gave him the feeling of a desired refuge" (p. 383). Once
again, art serves a central purpose in the life of a Laforet protagonist.
In *Nothing* art provides the format for recapturing past experience,
a self-discovery in retrospect; in *The Island and the Devils* it serves
as a youthful delusion and diversion from the world, an imaginary
reality left behind as maturity dawns; in *Sunstroke* the recognition
and acceptance of the importance of art is the mark of maturity, the
"dying into life" of the sensitive soul. The psychological depth and
its complex relation to social milieu that Laforet achieves in *The
New Woman* is present in *Sunstroke* and is treated with even greater
perspicacity, perhaps because Laforet is more comfortable portraying the world of adolescents. She adeptly handles the male/female
dichotomy that anchors the rambling series of actions, multiplying
and diversifying the theme from the vantage point of motherhood,
fatherhood, sibling relationships, and sexual relationships of the
widest possible variety.

IV *The Underlying Paradigm of the Four Novels:
Family Archetypes*

The role of the family in the structure and meaning of Carmen
Laforet's four long novels has been discussed peripherally in the

above sections. I now wish to extract this fundamental issue and arrive at some conclusions about its function in Laforet's novelistic canon. None of the novels employs traditional novelistic methods of developing actions, advancing characters in situations, or focusing on themes. The protagonists are seen at a crucial stage in their personal development; all other novelistic elements—secondary characters, ambience, etc.—are contingent upon highlighting aspects of this development. Since family role models (e.g., the mother/father polarity) are basic to psychological and social development, most secondary characters assume characteristics of parent models with regard to the protagonists.

All the novels have one feature in common: the protagonists are partially or wholly orphaned. In each case either the mother (or both parents) is dead or ineffectual, as in *The Island and the Devils*. Laforet says that she avoids the mother figure in her novels because she is boring, but there is perhaps a subconscious reason for Laforet's eliminating the carnal mother from her protagonists' lives; the exercise of mothering would have thwarted the underlying literary goal of each of these novels: successful personal exploration and growth. Each novel may be seen as a progression of confrontations with and eventual rejection of role models.

The orphans in each novel have a variety of inadequate substitute mother figures. In *Nothing*, Angustias is too strict and harsh; she lacks maternal warmth and understanding. A feminist critic shows how this aspect of Angustias makes her a paternal figure:

[Angustias] like Bernarda Alba . . . is [a] reinforcer of the most stagnant, reactionary and life-stifling realities of Spanish society. . . . She is more than "protector," "pseudo-protector" or "stepmother" figure, as an antiquated vestige from the past, she is enforcer of the most stringent and repressive aspects of partriarchal morality. Sexually frustrated herself, she becomes victim turned victimizer, a disturbing but typical example of how patriarchy enlists women, without their conscious knowledge, for the defense and enforcement of the established power structure.[4]

In the same novel, Ena's mother could have been a positive model for Andrea, but she loses credibility when she turns to Andrea for help with her own daughter, then engaged in a strange affair with Andrea's uncle. Andrea's aunt Gloria is so childish that Andrea often assumes a motherlike role as her confidant—a reversal of the adult-child relationship.

In *The Island and the Devils*, Marta's stepsister-in-law Pino, although older and married, is a useless role model, because she is restricted to a semimature state by her domineering husband and her own strong mother. Like Gloria, she is in many ways less adult than the adolescent protagonist; Pino is given to temper tantrums that put her to bed for days at a time. Marta turns to her aunt Matilde, an educated woman who writes poetry, but she is too wrapped up in Franco's Nationalist cause to pay attention to Marta. In *The New Woman*, Paulina's mother-in-law is a matriarch ruling over the family's members and holdings as though she were a man; she is incapable of understanding Paulina's sensitive nature. However, Blanca, the mother-in-law of Paulina's lover, becomes a spiritual mother to her after her conversion. And in one more variation, in *Sunstroke* Martín's stepmother is so upset by his presence that she becomes physically ill and cannot stand to have him in her sight.

The grandmothers (Andrea, Paulina, and Martín all live with grandmothers at some point in the novels) come closest to the nurturing mother role. But grandmothers are too removed in time by age and traditions to completely fill the motherhood role. They are too lenient, and in fact have not been very successful in raising their own children, the protagonists' parents, aunts, and uncles, all of whom display problematic personalities. A grandmother is blamed for the supermacho and thus socially and economically ineffective Román and Juan, Andrea's uncles, for Martín's father, Eugenio, who eventually rejects his own son for suspected homosexuality, for Marta's uncle Daniel, a hypochondriac, and for frustrated women like Angustias. Jung tells us that the mother archetype fulfills two roles in the psychic life of a person, the good mother role and the bad mother role. The good mother image is compassionate, nurturing, and protective; the bad mother is wicked and destructive. What is largely absent in Carmen Laforet's familial structure is the good mother figure, what Erich Neumann calls in *The Great Mother* " 'the sheltering structure' within which *all* the mysteries of life take place, 'preservation, formation, nourishment, and transformation.' "[5]

The bad mother role can emerge from the good mother's activities if carried to excess. The good mother may stifle the possibilities of risk and free choice for the child. According to Sven Armens in his book *The Archetype of the Family in Literature*, "the . . . Mother may love so strongly, so blindly, that [she] will smother rather than encourage growth. . . . Because love cannot control itself, it is thought that feminine impulse must be curbed by the reins of a controlling intellect lest it weaken the very foundations of social order."[6] A Jungian psychologist carries this limiting aspect of motherly love even further:

In all cultures, the labyrinth has the meaning of an entangling and confusing representation of the world of matriarchal consciousness; it can be traversed only by those who are ready for a special initiation into the mysterious world of the collective unconscious. Having overcome this danger, Theseus rescued Ariadne, a maiden in distress. This rescue symbolizes the liberation of the anima figure from the devouring aspect of the mother image.[7]

The two aspects of the mother figure are related to the two faces of nature as represented in myth and literature. Nature is creator and destroyer of its own creation. Motherhood, the feminine principle, and nature are associated with primeval chaos, while the masculine principle is related to organization and order.

A mother figure, a traditional nurturing model in Carmen Laforet's novels, would have been a deterrent to the action of the works, based on the vicissitudes of self-discovery. This maternal perversion of growth is exemplified in *Nothing* by the relationship between Ena and her mother. Ena's mother tells Andrea that she did not begin to live until Ena (her first child) was born; her very existence depends on that of her daughter. Ena, in turn, nearly sacrifices her happiness with Jaime by turning her back on her fiancé to pursue a relationship with Román, ostensibly to avenge his cruelty to her mother. Without the nurturing mother, who is also restricting and confining, the hero or heroine is free to embark on a journey of increasing self-awareness, and on his or her way he or she encounters possible mother substitutes, who serve as temporary good or bad mothers, good or bad parent models. In each case, in the absence of the archetypal mother or any worthy substitute, the protagonists seek the archetypal father, who superficially seems more readily at hand.

At first Andrea is attracted to Román, who has nearly supernatural powers as a musician, but Román is a demon, not a good father or God image. Andrea also gives up hope of being saved by Pons, her imaginary knight in shining armor. Pons is obviously too young and immature for Andrea's psychological needs. At the end of the novel,

Andrea goes to Madrid with Ena's father, the most traditional paternal figure in her life.

Marta, in *The Island and the Devils*, is attracted to Pablo, in a kind of adolescent hero worship. Though Marta does not recognize his defective masculinity, other characters point out that he isn't fighting in the Civil War because he is lame and that his wife has turned her back on him because she is involved with the Republican war effort. (Only women in this novel are at all interested in the war.) Pablo finally loses his power over Marta when she discovers his illicit relationship with her frivolous aunt Honesta. No positive father figure is forthcoming in Marta's life, but at the end of the novel she goes off to Madrid with her relatives, to a figurative patriarchy—the Nationalists have just won the war. The arch-Nationalist Matilde will represent masculine guidance in Marta's life: "Ever since she had learned that her niece was going with them, Matilde had begun to assume an authoritarian air with Marta" (*N*, pp. 627–28).

Paulina in *The New Woman* takes the paradigm a step further; she pledges herself to the spiritual archetypal father, God: "She turned to God, she lifted her heart to Him, and asked Him what he wished of her, poor woman that she was . . ." (*N*, p. 1145). The Freudian or Jungian intent of this conversion is thinly disguised. In her first confession as a new Christian, Paulina tells her rather stunned confessor: "When I was a little girl, I hated my father... I never confessed..." (*N*, p. 1148). She is quite aware of the masculine/feminine dichotomy in her relationship to the Church, which is run by men:

That that man, who had studied the science of God, had separated himself from everything that the world could offer him, for God; and he was a minister of God... And she, who was a woman who had just looked at the supernatural world for the first time... that they, two, who had never seen each other until then, loved each other deeply in the love of The One who had called them. (*N*, p. 1152)

Blanca is the archetypal female who supports Paulina in her conversion and stands in relation to the protagonist in much the same way that the Virgin did to the medieval faithful who went astray. According to Armens, the medieval monks attained "the infinite Father through the tender spiritual motherhood of Mary" (p. 20).

At the end of *The New Woman*, Paulina decides to return to her husband and son in the village and take up her domestic duties once again. It is as though after having adjusted her psychic life in an encounter with the archetypal father God, assisted by the archetypal mother, Mary, she is able to accept traditional roles for herself. Both Carmen Laforet and her critics have indicated that they find the ending of this novel forced. When the novelistic action is seen as based on a movement toward and away from the masculine and feminine polarities at different levels, Paulina's decision to return to Eulogio is more acceptable.

If *The New Woman* takes the masculine/feminine dichotomy to the level of Christian religion, *Sunstroke* moves it to the realm of classical mythology. Martín is a modern-day Icarus, figuratively burned by too much of the masculine element, metaphorically represented by the sun (often a masculine God image in primitive religions). Having no real mother and no adequate mother surrogate, he is left unprotected before the harsh hand of his supermasculine father. The father's constant preoccupation throughout the novel is that Martín is not man enough. When the father finds Martín's close friend Carlos asleep with him in his bed, he jumps to the obvious conclusion. Guilty or not, Martín is banished forever from his father's house. The father assumes the role of the relentless sun God or of the punishing Old Testament Jehovah:

. . . the Old Testament Jehovah, in His more extreme manifestations as the guardian of the Old Law, and the proponent of strict obedience to authority, is equated with the intense purity of the unsheathed sun, a force of all-consuming power. Images of destruction, especially those of fire, are now commonly accepted as symptomatic of a patriarchal solar orientation of the psyche.[8]

In all cases of the absent mother and the subsequent confrontation with the father figure in Laforet's novels, the experience is one of growth and maturation for the protagonists. Even in Martín's case, after being rejected by his father, he is free to pursue the artistic career for which he has talent. Professor Armens, once again, illuminates this process:

Confronted with this overwhelming strength in the figure of the father, the face of the child turns pale with fear and he cowers from the threatening storm, the raised hand. However, when this force becomes his mentor at the pubertal period of initiation, he experiences a new possibility. Suddenly, he is aware that he too can possess this power, he too can be as the river and the thunderbolt. The revelation of the strength latent within him, as it is demonstrated in the grown father, makes him seek guidance for his aspiration. Such guidance is not to be found in the matriarchal environs of the Physical Hearth, but is readily available if he will but heed his father's cry from the doorway of the Sacred Fire. It is a call to knowledge and power but it is also a call to pain. . . . Theoretically, the archetypal Father figures of masculine dominance manifest their control in two ways: through denying the expected paternal strength and assistance, and through assumption of the "right"to punish. Thus it is by taking the great step from a world of almost total acceptance to a world embodying demands and the possibility of rejection and punishment that we are led from the primordial Physical Hearth to the ancient Greek and Roman altars with their dominant symbol of the Sacred Fire.[9]

Erich Neumann in *The Origins and History of Consciousness* points out that women are not allowed to witness primitive rituals of puberty, signaling maturation of the adolescent. This prohibition seems to symbolize a breaking of the maternal bond that limits child development.

In conclusion, then, the absence of biological, and by extension archetypally perfect mothers, in Laforet's novels motivates her protagonists to seek alternative parent models. The basic theme of all her novels is the development of sexual identity at an archetypal level. The encounters with potential father figures, with partially good mothers, or with bad mothers constitute the experiences upon which the tension of Carmen Laforet's novels rests.

CHAPTER 5

The Short Fiction

M OST of Carmen Laforet's short fiction, including short stories and novelettes, was published in two volumes that reflect two different phases of her work. The stories served to keep the writer's craft active while she was preparing *The Island and the Devils*; the short novels had the same purpose with respect to *The New Woman*:

Between my first novel and the second, there was a silence of seven years. . . . During the first three years of this interval of seven, between novel and novel, I did not write anything at all for the public. Then I began to publish some articles and stories.[1]

These [short] novels came into being during the time I was thinking about and working out a new novel. They were born in the span of time between *The Island and the Devils* (1952) and *The New Woman* (1955).[2]

Although there is some overlapping in the chronology of the stories and novelettes, I will discuss the stories together as a group and the short novels as another discrete body of work.

I The Short Stories

The short stories, written for the most part between 1945 and 1952, were published in a volume bearing the title of one of the stories: *La muerta* (The Dead Woman); some of the stories in this volume had been published separately in journals. *The Dead Woman* contains the stories "Última noche" (The Last Night), "Rosamunda," "El regreso" (The Homecoming), "La fotografía" (The Photograph), "Al colegio" (Off to School), "En la edad del pato" (At the Awkward Age), "El veraneo" (The Summer Vacation), and "The Dead Woman." Two more stories originally published in a separate small volume are included with these in the *Complete Works*: "Un

matrimonio" (A Marriage) and "El aguinaldo" (The Christmas Gift).
These two stories differ markedly in theme from the earlier collected
stories and reflect Laforet's changed attitude toward human nature,
society, and religion after her conversion.

In discussing the stories, I have attempted to establish a chronological order based on the themes of those of known date, judging
the chronology of the others by analogy. We know for certain that
"The Last Night" is the earliest, having been written during Laforet's student days in Barcelona. In the prologue to *La niña* (The
Little Girl), a collection of some of the stories and three novelettes
published in 1970, she says that several of her favorite stories are
the early "Rosamunda" and "The Dead Woman," written much
later. With those data as a chronological skeleton, I have attempted
to establish the order of the other stories by subject and treatment.
The stories with the motherhood theme ("The Photograph" and
"Off to School") were likely written when Laforet's children were
quite young (between 1945 and 1951). Those centering on the Christian charity theme probably date from the conversion period
(1951–1956).

Laforet wrote several other stories published in journals, but
never collected. "El infierno" (The Inferno), a story based on a
miracle of the Virgin in the style of Gonzalo de Berceo, was published in *Ínsula* in 1944, the year Laforet was much in the public
eye for receiving the Nadal Prize. *Ínsula* also published "Recién
casados" (The Newlyweds) in 1954, a story with a decidedly feminist
perspective. "El alivio" (The Unburdening) appeared in the June
1953 issue of *Destino*, and *Bazar*, a children's magazine, published
Laforet's only patent piece of children's literature: "El secreto de
la gata" (The Cat's Secret) in the March 1952 issue. Since these
stories are not available in collections to the general public, I will
give detailed summaries of them at the end of this section along
with an appraisal of their merit. There are perhaps other uncollected
stories, but the author has not kept copies of all her stories and
articles, nor does she have a complete list of all her journal publications.

II *The Nine Collected Stories*

"Última noche" (The Last Night), Laforet's earliest collected story
and the only one that has a World War II setting, is surely the

weakest. Claude, a twenty-two-year-old war widow whose husband, Paul, was shot as a deserter, is portrayed on the eve before her departure with her son to live on the sunny southern coast of France with her husband's mother. She rereads her husband's diary in which he tells of his cowardly self-inflicted injury to escape the battlefields. In the pages of the diary, he also recalls his meeting Claude during his recovery leave and returning to the front fortified by love, determined to fight bravely and cleanse his sullied honor. The lieutenant in command refused him a leave to marry Claude when she wrote that she was pregnant, so Paul once again resorted to self-inflicted injury, but this time the lieutenant did not ignore his unsoldierly conduct, and Paul was executed. Claude burns the rest of the confession, but saves these few pages for her son, so that he may learn his father's story through his own words. The story material (the horrors of war) seems trite and romantically overdone (the night Claude reads the diary, it is gray and rainy), but Laforet is already beginning to show her talent for storytelling. The use of the second person throughout, except for the opening and closing segments, gives an intimacy of confession, a freshness and candor that will be one of the marks of distinction in *Nothing*.

"Rosamunda" develops a theme that surfaces repeatedly in Laforet's later fiction—the conflict between personal aspirations and the limits which social reality places on the fulfillment of those dreams. She approaches the theme kaleidoscopically from multiple perspectives in *The Island and the Devils* and reworks and elaborates the "Rosamunda" story in the novelette *La llamada* (The Vocation). "Rosamunda" is one of the brightest gems in Laforet's literary crown, because the theme of dashed hopes is treated with perhaps greater sensitivity and more narrative efficiency than in any of her other writings.

Rosamunda is a woman, bizarrely dressed in an ancient evening gown and ballet slippers, who tells her story to a young army officer in the early-morning hours as they travel on a third-class train. She relates her account in the third person. Her real name is Felisa, but she has always called herself Rosamunda, constructing an imaginary world for herself that shields her from the harsh realities of an uncouth husband, a cramped house, and a bleak life in a monotonous village. As she tells her story, she exaggerates her talent as a young actress and poetess, whose brilliant career was truncated by marriage. She affirms that she was married at sixteen (she was really twenty-three); the great adventures onstage she claims to have had before marriage were in reality nothing more than a few private poetry readings at a friend's house. She fantasizes on her recent fabulous successes in the city during her return to the stage after many years (actually she was reduced to eating with beggars). Her husband saved her from ridicule and starvation by writing her to return home. She pretends to comply with his wishes not out of necessity, but because he is the father of her favorite child, whimsically named Florisel. Florisel, the only one of her children to believe her artistic pretensions, is now dead. The story ends with a delicate touch of irony. The young soldier, who reminds Rosamunda of Florisel, invites the crazy old lady to have breakfast with him at the station and begins to imagine how he will tell his friends about the beautiful young starlet he met on the train and with whom he had breakfast. The succinctly and poignantly stated message is that life is more bearable when the imagination is used to distort reality. And the success of its narration lies in the brevity and contrapuntal, conversational technique. Richness and depth are achieved economically in the names Rosamunda/Felisa and Florisel and by having the young soldier enter into Rosamunda's world (in his own way), rather than standing apart with a harsh, realistic eye.

"El veraneo" (The Summer Vacation) treats a theme similar to that of "Rosamunda," but in a much more pessimistic and less warmly human fashion. Rosa, the young woman sacrificed in this story, does not have the refuge of fantasy. Rosa's family spent their meager funds for educating their children on the son, Juan Pablo, whom they thought had talent for writing. After Juan Pablo had become successful, it was assumed, he would rescue his sister from her unsuitable post as a village schoolteacher and pay for her education in the city. Ten years have passed and Juan Pablo has yet to achieve the aspirations his sister and parents had for him; Rosa is still a village schoolteacher. The story centers on Juan Pablo's visit to his sister in the village, which is to be a summer vacation for him, away from the cares of the city where he is trying to establish himself as a writer (actually he sits in cafés most of the time, conversing with friends).

The affectionate display between brother and sister at the beginning of the story (Rosa maternally shoos her brother out of the house for a walk among the pleasantly described, peaceful surroundings of the village) is countered by the ironic revelation of Rosa's sacrifice and the underlying monotony of "peaceful" village life. The irony derives from two sources: (1) comments the brother makes to Rosa directly about the peasantlike appearance she has taken on in the years she has spent in the village, and (2) a conversation Juan Pablo has with the village doctor, whom he meets during his walk about the town. The doctor, a former suitor of Rosa's, pretends not to know Juan Pablo's relationship to the schoolteacher and launches into a description of her tragedy: her interests and talents having been subordinated to those of a less-talented brother, her exile in the village, her having refused marriage with the doctor because she always believed her brother would save her from village life.

The doctor gradually undermines the pompous self-esteem Juan Pablo had shown at the beginning of the story. Juan Pablo silently expiates his own guilt as he becomes increasingly irritated with the doctor; he thinks to himself: "If the girl really had backbone, she would have left the village without assistance from him or anybody... Ah! He too had suffered hunger, something Rosa did not know... He felt like telling this doctor a thing or two" (*N*, p. 280). As Juan Pablo returns to Rosa's house after the disagreeable encounter with the doctor, he decides to leave the village the next day and return to Madrid, thus ending after only a day and a half his projected monthlong stay in the country.

"The Summer Vacation" is a milestone in Laforet's use of indirect narrative focus to reveal a painful truth in all its ambiguity, a technique used with success in *The Island and the Devils*. The story is also a concentrated statement of a thorny moral problem: Where does responsibility lie—in the individual or with society—for the individual's success or failure to realize personal dreams and potential? Rosa does not blame her brother for her unfulfilled potential, but clearly the doctor does. Juan Pablo attempts, unconvincingly, to rationalize away his responsibility and place it on his sister. None of the solutions to the problem of moral responsibility is satisfying, and the story remains appropriately elusive and ambiguous.

"El regreso" (The Homecoming) may not form a chronological unit with stories discussed to this point, but they do form a thematic and narrative whole. All four stories deal with the themes of human frailty and lost illusions in a delicate but decidedly ironic fashion.

In each case the irony derives from the complexity of the narrative technique, which projects an oblique perspective on the situation. In "The Homecoming" Julián is released from a mental institution just in time to spend Christmas Eve with his family. He has grave doubts about leaving the protection of the institution to return to the harsh world of family responsibilities and obligations; he even suggests to one of the sisters that he be allowed to stay, at least until the next day: "that place of death and desperation [the hospital] had been for him, Julián, a good refuge, a good salvation..." (N, p. 315). His wish is granted at the last moment, when his wife is prevented from coming to get him by illness in the family.

He arrives home on the train the next day, Christmas Day. The train ride gives Julián time to think about his home and life with his family during the winter before his loss of reason. He was out of work; his wife, pregnant with yet another child, scrubbed floors in order to buy food (mostly watery soup). Julián buys a cake in a pastry shop as he walks home from the train station; he feels embarrassed at having eaten so many pastries in the sanatorium the night before, imagining that his family has done without. When he arrives at his apartment, he is confronted with the unexpected scene of a well-laid table full of holiday treats. His wife explains that during his absence the family became objects of charity, so they were actually better off during his absence. While his wife also explains that the charitable ladies will find work for Julián, the full weight of the responsibilities to which he has returned descends upon him:

Again, with their hands, they pointed out to him the basket full of gifts, the eager and enthused faces of the children. To him, that thin man, with his black coat and bugging eyes, who was so sad, it was as though, on that Christmas Day, he had left infancy anew in order to see with all the cruelty once again, under those gifts, the same old life of before. (N, pp. 319–20)

The hunger theme and the social suffering that were so much a part of Spanish life in the 1940s and that were always present in the background of Nothing are here reflected from the dual mirror of Julián's viewpoint, but told in the third person. The reader sympathizes with Julián's plight and his desire not to face reality but, being privy to Julián's conscience and self-condemnation for cowardice, the reader's sympathy is thwarted and confused. Once more Laforet achieves moral complexity through narrative skill.

"La fotografía" (The Photograph) is part of another thematic group of stories reflecting the concerns of motherhood, of which Laforet often wrote in her newspaper articles during 1951 and 1952. In them she abandons the narrative irony of the earlier stories, shifting to a more unified voice that extols tenderness, self-sacrifice, and love. In "The Photograph" the protagonist, Leonor, whose husband is exiled after the war, is struggling to raise their child alone by giving classes. She dreams of saving enough money to send her husband a photograph of herself with the child. This story is somewhat longer than many of the others as Laforet carefully builds the penurious situation in which Leonor lives to contrast it with the anticlimactic moment when the photograph is finally taken. Leonor buys only one orange a day from the fruit seller—for her child; she does not permit herself the luxury of eating fruit. Her life is a continual frenzy of giving classes, shopping, maintaining a household and child.

Finally the day arrives when she has the necessary fifty *pesetas* for the photographic sitting. The blasé, unconcerned attitude of the photographer and her assistant contrasts sharply with the expectation that has been building in Leonor. In fact the photographers treat her with contempt when she requests a photograph of their faces only. She cannot afford the full-length view she had hoped for. Leonor's disappointment at this detail seems much more meaningful than that of the photographers, to whom it means making a few *pesetas* less on the sitting; she had spent money unnecessarily to buy the baby a new suit, and she has carefully ironed her own dress for the full-length pose. During the sitting, the lady photographer Doña María is occupied with her own problems, because business has fallen off since her husband died. The sitting is over in a moment. When Leonor leaves, the assistant complains that for such a cheap photograph she could have come earlier in the day and not have ruined their tranquil Sunday afternoon. In contrast to Leonor's frantic but purposeful life, Doña María will be left alone in her house, when the assistant leaves, "with the great machine covered in black and with the forced smile of the unknown portraits hanging on the walls" (*N*, p. 292). Laforet juxtaposes the lives of two women struggling to make ends meet alone; Leonor seems heroic, while Doña María's life is sad and vacuous. The message here, that the most rewarding life is the one in which there is moral purpose and commitment, particularly to family and children, is also the message of *The New Woman*.

"Al colegio" (Off to School) is one of Laforet's favorites among her own work. It really is not a story in the true sense of an artfully related, fictitious incident with a well-defined rhythm of beginning, middle, and end. It is classified in *Mis páginas mejores* (My Best Pages), where it is collected along with several other stories, novelettes, and excerpts of novels, as an *estampa* (vignette). What removes it from the short-story category is its truly autobiographical, nonfictional character. The narrative voice is that of Carmen Laforet, with no intervening artistic qualifier. "Off to School" has exactly the same focus and tone of Laforet's newspaper articles, "Puntos de vista de una mujer" (From a Woman's Point-of-view), in *Destino* and "Diario de Carmen Laforet" (Diary of Carmen Laforet) in *ABC*. Perhaps it was first written as a journal piece, and when Laforet realized its literary merit she decided to include it with the stories.

"Off to School" depicts a young mother taking her little daughter to school for the first time, from the mother's point of view. It begins with the mother/narrator and her daughter walking hand-in-hand through the streets. At first there seems to be nothing unusual about this particular day. They pass a taxi stand, which reminds the mother of past outings with her daughter. They almost always take a taxi, then go to the park, and eat ice cream, chatting as they go. But today they pass the taxis without stopping; they are going to school and will arrive there by a complicated route without a taxi. The mother removes her glove in order to feel the sensation of her daughter's hand. They communicate their mutual excitement and apprehension by subtly changing the pressures of their hands. They finally arrive at the school. The moment the little girl leaves her mother and moves toward the group of smallest children, the mother has the sensation that her daughter has begun her own life. She understands that while her daughter grows in the world of her own work, friends, and illusions, she will become a person separate from her, but in her heart they will be united. This fusion and transformation will occur because the mother will relive her own girlhood in that of the daughter:

But I wish that someone would explain to me why, as I am walking along the sidewalk, spotted with sun and mist, and hearing the school bell calling in the class, why, I say, do I have this anxious expectation, this joy, why do I imagine the classroom and the window, and my little desk, from which I see the garden, and I even see clearly, emotionally, a huge A drawn on the blackboard with yellow chalk, which is the first letter I am going to learn... (*N*, p. 313)

The vignette is masterfully developed to allow the psychology of the child at this moment to be overlayed with the mother's perspective. The narrator/mother projects the dual vision.

"En la edad del pato" (The Awkward Age) also describes a moment of childhood schooldays from an adult perspective, capturing with the irony of a mature eye the camaraderie between young girls at the pubertal age. The narration in third-person plural contributes to the sense of collectiveness important at that stage in life. In the group of girls that is the collective protagonist, Cristina, more clever than the others, invents a contest: her classmates must guess the identities of persons she has drawn in the form of animals. The participants in the contest are to receive prizes by raffle. The whole idea was inspired when Cristina recognized in a drawing of an owl the likeness of one sad, withdrawn little girl in the class, always dressed in mourning clothes. During the contest, the owllike girl recognizes her own caricature and participates in the raffle. Cristina has chosen the prizes from her girlish possessions. When the sad little girl does not win anything, Cristina says that her number has also won a prize and generously gives her a favorite possession, a new pen. "Owlie" receives the sacrificed pen without smiling, as something that is her due. Cristina recognizes the cruelty of her owl drawing and tries to rectify with the spurious prize, but the damage has been done. Contrary to many stories (real and invented) about children's unfeeling cruelty to one another, this little tale marks the age at which children are becoming adults, a process which includes assuming moral responsibility for one's actions toward others. Here are reflected the ethical concerns introduced into the adolescent initiation ritual, which are lacking in Laforet's first two novels, but which are central to the last one.

"La muerta" (The Dead Woman) forms an ideological unit with "The Marriage," "A Christmas Gift," *The New Woman*, and the novelettes, all exemplifying a Christian charity and sacrifice probably related to Carmen Laforet's conversion in December of 1951.

"The Dead Woman" narrates a woman's silent suffering throughout a life of illness and pain, told from the point of view of her husband three weeks after her death. During his life with his wife, Don Paco had been resentful of his wife's incapacities (she was even paralyzed for a time); their house was never in good order, and the two daughters fought constantly over which one of them was to do the small amount of housework that was accomplished. Don Paco consoled himself with fantasies of the time when his wife would finally be dead; he could ask his daughters to leave the house and perhaps take up with the handsome widow next door. When the dreamed-of moment arrives, and his wife finally does die, the daughters miraculously become more tidy and cooperative. Don Paco finds that he no longer desires the freer life he had been looking forward to; his thoughts now turn frequently to his dead wife, and he lives with his memories of her rather than with the handsome widow. He thinks of his wife as a saint, understanding that the meaning of her life (seemingly so useless while she was alive) was to be a kind of consolation and peace-making agency to her family after her death.

"The Dead Woman" is one of Laforet's most accomplished short pieces. Much of its success arises from the sense of space created in the house. The story begins with Don Paco's entry into the hallway of the house after work; he seems to smell something, a sensation of the dead woman's presence. He feels her proximity "in the quiet hallway of the house, in the ray of sunlight that squeezed in through the little window and fell on the red tiles of the hall floor" (N, p. 266). His mind drifts back to the early days of his marriage, before his wife's illness destroyed his happiness. Even when she became ill, he believed she continued to be perfectly happy as long as she had her medicines; she did not seem to realize how unfulfilled his life was. He ironically reflects on how certain he was that she never suffered, because she never complained. His memories center on typical scenes in the house, thus juxtaposing the past and the present in the same significant space. As Don Paco's mind returns to the present, he is aware of the heat of the sun in the hallway and the fresh cleanliness of the kitchen. The pleasant retreat into which the house has been transformed since María's death is a fine metaphor for the meaning of her patient, suffering life. Carmen Laforet is at her narrative zenith in *Nothing* and in stories such as "Rosamunda" and "The Dead Woman," wherein she welds memory and truth into a fictive unit.

Marriage as sacrifice is the theme of a number of Laforet's narratives. In the short story "Un matrimonio" (A Marriage), Pedro, a wealthy playboy student, gives up his inheritance in order to marry Gloria, his showgirl mistress, after she becomes pregnant. Even though Pedro's parents have told him that in marrying Gloria he has ceased to exist for them, Gloria encourages him to send the parents a telegram when their child is born. The night the story takes place, Pedro has just received the reply from his parents, reaffirming their rejection of their son and grandchild. He is in the streets, hungry and cold (having sold his good winter coat to get food for Gloria). As he tears up the telegram from his father and drops it on the ground, he finds a twenty-five *peseta* piece, which allows him to have his first decent meal in days.

On returning to the apartment he shares with Gloria and a renter, Gloria informs him joyfully that there is a letter offering him work as a bricklayer's assistant. Pedro becomes slightly depressed, as he is unaccustomed to hard physical labor and finds it almost overwhelmingly exhausting. During his conversation with Gloria, he watches her with the child and a strong emotion of love and purpose in life comes over him. He begins to feel less pessimistic about the misery he will have to endure in taking on the responsibility of a wife and child. The sense of despair and hopelessness evident in the male provider of "The Homecoming" is here transformed into the joy of simple, basic human pleasures. However, Gloria's final remark to Pedro (she calls him a "poet" and "dreamer") as he talks of their life together sheds a bit of irony on Pedro's rosy vision of the future. Even in her most Christian and charitable moments, Carmen Laforet is unwilling to reduce her moral view of the world to a simple "Be humble and God will provide." Life is too complex for that, and her fictional microcosms reflect the ironies and complexities of moral living.

"El aguinaldo" (The Christmas Gift) is surely the most Christian of all Laforet's works, and it is the least ironic. Significantly, it is one of only two stories taking place on religious holidays. (The holidays are used as mileposts in all of the novels.) The story portrays a mini-conversion, the religious experience of a woman whose life was empty and meaningless before a brief encounter with a kind of lay saint or martyr. There is a custom in Dr. López-Gay's hospital that the doctors' wives take gifts of sweets to the patients in their husbands' wards on Christmas Eve. Much to Dr. López-Gay's consternation, his pregnant wife refuses to go this year; his ward contains mostly insane people, and his wife does not feel up to that unpleasant spectacle. Doctor López-Gay believes his reputation will suffer, so finally his young-looking, stylish mother-in-law, Isabel, agrees to go. As Isabel enters the chauffeured car to be driven to the hospital, she remembers how empty her life is; she has been experiencing a strange sense of meaninglessness for some time: "Love comes and goes. Children grow up and disillusion one..." (N, p. 337). With these thoughts she passes the time on the way to the hospital. Her son-in-law's ward is truly depressing. The insane women, all of them deformed in some way, fight over the candy gifts.

Isabel asks for Manuela Ruiz, a limp rag of a woman, completely paralyzed with her head fastened to a board so that it will not fall forward. She has a terrible scar that runs from her mouth to her chin, formed by the steady trickle of saliva that has dripped from her paralyzed mouth for years. Isabel realizes from the compassionate look in Manuela's eyes that this unfortunate creature feels sorry for *her* (Isabel), having to witness such a sight. The doctor has sent a volume of San Juan de la Cruz's poetry to Manuela. Although Manuela cannot read, others often read to her—mostly religious books. Through her religious readings, Manuela has come to understand (she has been hospitalized for forty years) what God intended for her life. Because she has nothing and can do nothing, she is completely free to pray and devote herself to helping others through prayer.

A nun relates to Isabel that her son-in-law, whom Isabel had always thought vulgar, often sits with Manuela because his spirit soars just being near her. Isabel's opinion of her son-in-law is transformed, as is her attitude toward her own life; her emptiness lifts. The entire family notices the transformation when she returns from the hospital, and a feeling of warmth and well-being pervades the house: "Just a few hours earlier Isabel had been filled with melancholy; now a warm happiness filled her in that comfortable living room, among those people who were worthy of being loved" (N, p. 344).

III   *The Collected Stories in Perspective*

From the more pessimistic earlier stories to the optimistically Christian narratives of the early 1950s Laforet relies, for the effect of her stories, on creation of ambience and artistically appropriate narrative focus. She achieves the human warmth and sense of truth about life by placing her characters in their most basic living situation: Don Paco is in the hallway and the kitchen of the house he shared with his wife in "The Dead Woman"; Rosa in "The Summer Vacation" looks out the doorway of her house at "the handful of houses in the village"; Leonor in "The Photograph" walks hurriedly through the streets, pausing briefly at the flower stand and the window of the photographer's shop: "It was the hour when Leonor felt freer, more herself. That time of walking through the streets in the sun belonged to her and she enjoyed it completely" (*N*, p. 283). Julián presses his head against the window panes of the sanatorium at the beginning of the story; he goes from one kind of internment to another: "There were four uneven doors, which used to be painted green. One of them was his [to his apartment]" (*N*, p. 319). The two interior places in Julián's life are bridged by a brief view of the world outside: "The road to his house gleamed with display windows, shining with bakeries" (*N*, p. 318). The outside is glittery and brilliant, the inside grim with insanity or insanity-provoking hunger and responsibility.

The streets are Pedro's milieu in "A Marriage": "He began to enter now the illuminated streets, crossed by people well-wrapped up in their coats, and he felt ashamed to be talking to himself" (*N*, p. 323). Characters in Laforet's works often find walking in the streets the appropriate place to reflect on their lives and advance their understanding of their situations. Laforet uses both external ambience and interiors to accompany the near-miraculous transformation of Isabel in "A Christmas Gift." The story begins with Dr. López-Gay's house seen from the outside on a gray morning: "On Christmas Day dawn nearly did not break over that small, cold city crushed by a gray sky. At ten o'clock in the morning, in Doctor López-Gay's house the electric light could be seen shining behind the glass of some windows" (*N*, p. 334). The interior of the hospital is equally grim, with dirty, unpleasant smells. All this contrasts with the interior of the López-Gay house when Isabel returns from the hospital, the first time the house is seen from the inside. A fire warms the ambience both literally and symbolically, and now the

window panes separating the interior and exterior are seen from
the warm interior perspective: "And all of them looked toward the
window through which one could see the white marvels of the snow"
(*N*, p. 344).

IV   *The Uncollected Stories*

"El infierno" (The Inferno) appeared in the first issue (1944) of
the now well-respected Spanish literary monthly *Ínsula*, introduced
with a photograph, captioned "Carmen Laforet, author of the novel,
Nothing." One readily suspects that the new journal was eager to
capitalize upon this author's recent success and perhaps requested
she write something for them or submit some of her unpublished
work. Either because it was a youthful effort or an occasional piece,
"The Inferno" is unoriginal and stylistically immature. In the story,
a young monk hallucinates about the Virgin during a long night of
fever, presumed to be his last. As he kneels before a statue of the
Virgin in his cell, his life passes before his feverish eyes in the form
of little miniature paintings like those in religious books depicting
the lives of the saints. He remembers how as a boy, looking at
images and statues of the Virgin, he had fallen in love with her, not
as a spiritual, religious figure but as a corporeal woman. He confessed his sin formally, but fell into disgrace again by imaginatively
transforming a girlfriend into the Holy Mother; when he kissed the
real girl, he imagined himself kissing the religious idol.

He undertakes penance by traveling to Rome, praying constantly,
and finally giving up his fortune to become a monk. He hoped only
for some sign from the Virgin that she had forgiven his sins, but
she always remained impassive; to him she has a bitter, ironic smile.
On this night of his supposed death, he asks for the bejeweled
Virgin of the main altar to be brought to him as a last wish, still
hoping for the ultimate forgiveness. But he admits in his wild mental
ravings that rather than ask her for pardon, when she arrives he
will kiss her eyes, lips, and body. After admitting the sacrilege, a
silence falls over the room, and the monk feels a hand caressing his
head. It is the bejeweled Virgin, whom he begins to caress. She
seems to offer her lips. Finally he pauses to ask, "—Is this Hell..."
And the image responds, "—Do you prefer Heaven?... I give you
what you wanted, because I am the Sweet One, the Merciful, the
Generous... I am...." As he begins to kiss her again she disappears,

and he is left alone with the crude wooden Virgin of his cell, smiling at him with her ironic expression.

The monk does not die, whereupon the abbot proclaims a miracle of the Virgin. But the monk lives a long life of Hell on earth, since he has already attained his Heaven—his carnal desire for the Virgin. Thus the story inverts the kind of miracle of the Virgin recounted by the thirteenth-century poet Gonzalo de Berceo, in which a monk is truly saved from his sinful ways through the intervention of the Virgin. Laforet's story was perhaps influenced by Berceo as well as by the works of earlier twentieth-century Spanish novelists like Ramón Pérez de Ayala (*A.M.D.G.*) or Gabriel Miró (*Niño y grande, El obispo leproso*), where one also finds accounts of images of the Virgin provoking sensual feelings in young boys educated in strict monastery schools. The boys' natural sexual awakening is heightened by the vivid descriptions of the potential crimes and their punishments proffered in the religious lessons, and, having no normal sexual outlets in their rigid puritanical ambience, they become obsessed with the Virgin.

Some of the narrative techniques Laforet uses in later works are already in evidence here, particularly the tendency to transform a literary scene into a work of the plastic arts. The dying monk's cell "illuminated by the reddish glow of the candles, that night had the static enchantment of a retable." The details of the retable are then elaborated: the monk praying to the Virgin is positioned in the center surrounded by scenes from his life portrayed in artistic miniatures. The tendency to an ornate Baroque style in the story, while rather clumsily executed, heightens the sense of artistic elaboration which is finally more important than the story's trite theme. Every noun is accompanied by at least one adjective; metaphors and similes abound, as do heavily wrought turns of phrase such as "Some [images] come with the crushing sound of the gold of autumn leaves." This curious early story, which seems by its theme to stand outside the rest of Laforet's literary canon, could in retrospect prophesy her own religious crisis.

The ironic vision of marriage, or more particularly of men, found in "Recién casados" (The Newlyweds) suggests that it might have been written at the same time as the short novel "El noviazgo" (The Engagement). Both pieces, perhaps written earlier than the stories and novelettes of Laforet's "Catholic" period, seem to contradict the more positive view of marriage tendered in "Un matrimonio" (A Marriage) or "El piano" (The Piano), for example. In "The New-lyweds" a young wife's husband has just been transferred to Madrid from a provincial town where they had presumably met and spent the first months of their marriage. The wife (the narrator in the story) begins by confessing to be bored with her life in the capital; she as yet has no friends and her husband, preoccupied with his new managerial position, talks of nothing but his work. She longs to return to the provinces, "where there is time to read, to think, and even to daydream about the delicious life full of hustle and bustle that one would have in Madrid, if one only lived there." But she will not divulge her dissatisfaction to her husband, because he is pleased with the promotion he has received upon transferring to Madrid. In this seemingly extraneous manner Laforet subtly intro-duces the gulf in communication that already exists between this young woman and her husband of only a few months.

The story itself centers on an incident that illustrates this lack of communication, even subterfuge, in which the couple (particularly the wife) engages. Every afternoon the wife meets her husband at his office, and they go to a movie or take a stroll through the city streets. One day she enters the office as usual and encounters a strained atmosphere; her husband has just reprimanded a young man in his employ, Paco Álvarez, for falling behind in his work (the wife has found in the young man the only person she can converse with in Madrid, because, unlike her husband, Paco does not always talk of business). Before her marriage, the wife was more aggressive and would have interceded to defend the young man with whom she sympathizes, but now she pretends not to notice the strained situation.

After the woman and her husband leave the office, they go to a tea shop. To their embarrassment, they discover after consuming the tea and cookies that neither has brought any money. They discard the idea of one's leaving to go home (on the other side of the city) and decide instead to call Paco Álvarez, who is still working at the office, to come to their rescue. The husband phones, and Paco promises to come if he can obtain enough change; he says it is the end of the month, and his funds are low. The couple waits an inordinate amount of time; all the other patrons of the tea shop leave, and finally the head waiter approaches their table to remind them that closing time is 9:00. They say they are waiting for a friend, and the polite waiter allows them to remain. Their embarrassment could not be more acute, when finally Paco arrives with the money (which he says he has had some difficulty in collecting). The husband's attitude toward his "lazy" employee changes completely from his earlier anger; he greets Paco with the greatest cordiality and invites him to dine with them. Later at home alone with his wife, the husband praises Paco Álvarez for his virtues.

The wife recalls with irony that Paco had confided to her at the restaurant, while her husband was getting his coat, that he had lied about not having sufficient funds and had deliberately delayed coming to the tea shop. He wished to punish his employer for his cruelty earlier in the day by making him suffer embarrassment and discomfort. Paco was certain that the wife had understood his scheme and wished to apologize for making her suffer as well. She had, in fact, not seen through Paco's plot, but decides to accept Paco's compliment to her intelligence and not cause further unpleasantness between the two men by revealing Paco's revenge upon her husband. The story ends with the young woman wishing she had a female friend her own age in whom she could confide "how infantile men are." However pessimistic the message of the story may be for the possibility of real communication between members of the opposite sex, the ironic wit of the telling softens the pessimism and does not leave the reader with any sense of impending tragedy. The young woman will doubtless acquire friends in whom to confide, and she will probably settle into life in Madrid, involved in her own concerns.

"El alivio" (The Unburdening) focuses for its central theme on the plight of upper- and middle-class Spaniards who attempt to maintain social pretenses even when their financial circumstances no longer permit. (This problem is a leitmotif in the novels and in many of the other pieces of short fiction.) Herminia (aged forty) and her widowed mother now live respectably, but economically, in a suite of guest rooms at a convent, which they have furnished with a few fine things remaining to them from more abundant times. Mother and daughter decide to relive their former life for an afternoon by inviting several other ladies of similar circumstances to tea. As they indulge in the preparations—polishing silver and laying out the cookies on the table—it becomes evident that Herminia's mother has always considered her daughter's social graces much

116   CARMEN LAFORET

less refined than her own. She constantly harps at Herminia to
correct the fit of her dress, repowder her nose, not to walk like a
stick, and to refrain from making her usual infelicitous comments
in front of their guests. Herminia defers to her mother's superior
social elegance at every rebuke.

The idea of having guests had originally been Herminia's; she
had suggested repaying some kindnesses of their friend the marchioness by inviting her to tea. The mother had seized upon the
idea and expanded it into a formal tea party with other ladies included as well. The guests arrive and scrutinize the detailed preparations for the afternoon—the flower arrangements, the table cloth,
the displays of cookies on porcelain plates. The social pleasantries
begin: "—This was a wonderful idea on your part; so kind of you
to invite us." The conversation soon turns to earlier days when
these widows were young girls with hopes of making good marriages. They tease and flatter one another by recalling all the young
men interested in each one. Herminia has heard these same for-
mulaic conversations so often that she knows exactly what each lady
will say next. When the marchioness chides Herminia's mother for
trying to steal her suitors, Herminia nearly answers for her mother
because she has heard the reply so many times: "I remember the
dress you wore to the dance, Matilde; you were ravishing that day
when you went out on the dance floor with the general..."

Suddenly after several more polite exchanges of this kind, Herminia's mother breaks the ritual code by declaring that the marchioness actually never had any suitors; she was too ugly. In utter
shock Herminia spills tea on one of the guests, breaking the tension
for a moment. But her mother resumes her tirade: "You're all
ugly. . . . We called Mrs. Torrenegra the boring fly. . . ." The
horrified guests indignantly get up to leave as the mother continues
to rail at them, and Herminia attempts to calm mother and guests
alike. As the pitch of the mother's discourse grows, she punctuates
it by saying she feels great relief and whoops, "Tararí." At this point
the guests realize she is having an attack of insanity, and they begin
to view her with pity rather than dismay. They help Herminia
restrain her as she attempts to throw some of the silverware out
the window. Everyone, including Herminia, seems greatly relieved
to conclude that the mother has gone crazy; they view her madness
as natural after all she has suffered so heriocally in her life (e.g.,
covering up the penury of her existence). Thus each member of the

gathering undergoes an unburdening: the mother has broken the narrowly confining social rules she struggles to uphold, Herminia is relieved to see disappear the model of social grace to which she is constantly compared, and the guests have enjoyed an unusual event in their otherwise monotonous lives. The theme of truth told by an insane person is not particularly new, but Laforet has mastered her storytelling technique in this piece, building the tension nicely by using passages of indirect and direct dialogue to carry the momentum of the narration.

"El secreto de la gata" (The Cat's Secret), perhaps Laforet's only published children's story, seems to be a mature recollection of one of those tales she told her brothers as a girl. It is autobiographical in that the characters' names are hers and those of her brothers, and it includes the dream motif she used to introduce her childhood fabrications in order to make the story seem real rather than made up. Three children, Eduardo, Juan, and Carmen, live in a house full of animals—a chicken coop with hens; a turkey named Mr. Whisky; a watchdog, Numa, that belongs to the eldest brother, Eduardo; a lamb, Miguelete, belonging to Juan; and the youngest child, Carmen, has a cat, Pachota. Carmen is less adventuresome than her brothers, who frequently scale the wall surrounding their yard to venture into the yard of the abandoned house next door. Juan returns with tales of strange laments and even ghostly piano-playing in that neighboring house. These stories capture little Carmen's imagination, and she begins to notice that her cat, Pachota, frequently scales the wall into the adjacent yard as do many other cats in the neighborhood; they all disappear into the house.

One day Pachota, proclaiming herself queen of the cats, promises to take Carmen to the house next door that afternoon. Pachota explains that the red house next door is the house of the cats; the laments Juan heard are their conversations. The normally timid Carmen valiantly scales the wall as her brothers often do. What Pachota had said is true; the house is full of cats, who all greet their queen. Pachota climbs up on the piano and begins to play a strange sleep-inducing music. Carmen drifts off into slumber, only to awaken in her own bed at home with Pachota sitting at the foot, looking at her mysteriously, as if warning her not to disclose the secret she has learned. Carmen feels the satisfaction of having an animal superior to those of her brothers and of keeping a secret from them. From this one fine example of Laforet's ability to transform child psychology, mild sibling rivalry, into imaginative literature, one can only wish that she had employed her skill in other stories and books for children. Her storytelling talent was doubtless often used with her own children, several of whom have displayed literary interests themselves. Cristina translates English and American literature into Spanish, Silvia is involved in filmmaking, and the youngest son, in his late teens, has written short fiction.

Although the nine collected stories and four uncollected ones vary widely in subject matter, technique, purpose, and literary merit, all attest to a talent for storytelling, an ability to focus on a human event, however inconsequential, conveying substance and magnitude through a fortunate choice of words. This, of course, is part of the achievement of the novels and the novelettes as well. Laforet's qualities as a storyteller are probably best suited to the short novel, which I will discuss next. The novelette allows a fuller elaboration of the storytelling technique, without requiring the complex manipulation of plot, generic to the novel.

V *The Short Novels*

Carmen Laforet has written seven short novels, a genre she considers underrated. In her prologue to these seven novelettes in the collected works, she points to the great writers who have cultivated the short novel, especially Chekhov and Andreyev. The short novel, she believes, should not be thought a minor art—the art lies entirely in the genius of the writer, regardless of length or genre: "For me the long novel is where I concentrate the great, slow work of something that interests me deeply. Short novels have, in spite of this, a technique that is different from the story; they need a more solid plot structure, but their length in number of pages has depended, for me—as with the articles—upon editorial necessities" (*N*, p. 639).

As in the later short stories, the themes of charity and self-sacrifice predominate in most of the short novels: "La llamada" (The Vocation), "El último verano" (The Last Summer), "Un noviazgo" (An Engagement), and "El piano" (The Piano) were published independently under the umbrella title *The Vocation. Novelas* (Novels) includes three other short novels, all written in 1952 and 1953: "Los emplazados" (The Condemned), "El viaje divertido" (The Pleasure Trip), and "La niña" (The Little Girl). The first two are adapted from anecdotes Laforet had gathered earlier in her life and so do not reflect her involvement with Christianity to the degree that those in *The Vocation* do. "The Little Girl," however, centers on the life of a religiously oriented woman, who sacrifices her self-interest for her social duties. Many of the novelettes, with their extended format, include references to the ambience of Spanish life in the early 1950s. Character situation is not reduced to the physical space so important in the stories, but comprehends a wider variety of personal and social circumstances.

"The Vocation" is a longer and more complex elaboration of the "Rosamunda" plot. In some ways it is less successful than the short story, which gains its impact from the narrative technique of Rosamunda's recapitulation of her life during one early morning on the train. In "The Vocation," Mercedes's attempted return to the stage is narrated by a third person in an ongoing present, rather than in retrospect by the failed artist herself. The striking narrative irony of the story is thus absent in the novelette. In addition the narrative focus of the novelette is unnecessarily complicated at the outset by introducing a viewpoint that is then dropped and never reintroduced. Mercedes's decision to leave her family to fulfill her lifelong dreams of becoming a stage personality is stimulated by the sudden appearance of a friend who knew her in her youth, when she was still a beautiful, talented young girl. The story begins from the point of view of the friend, Don Juan. Old-fashioned-looking, out of place in the modern setting of the boat on which he is traveling, Don Juan disembarks for the day in a village and recognizes in a café waiter's face a familial resemblance to a friend of his youth. The young man is in fact the friend's grandson. Don Juan then decides to visit his friend's daughter, the waiter's mother, whom he recalls was very pretty and who wanted to go on the stage some twenty-five years before. Her family forced her to marry an insensitive man just to keep her from the stage.

Mercedes is now unkempt, has lost her beauty, and is even missing a tooth that her husband knocked out in an argument. Don Juan is horrified at the transformation, but sympathizes with her and tries to lift her spirits by telling her that she still has a beautiful voice for recitation. He gives her some money as he leaves. With this small encouragement and the money, Mercedes takes heart and decides to run away to the city to belatedly fulfill her career dreams. After thus setting the action in motion, Don Juan disappears and is never mentioned again.

In the city, Mercedes counts on the help of the only relative who opposed her unsuitable marriage—her sister's mother-in-law. The sister is now dead, and the mother-in-law lives with a granddaughter. The old lady receives Mercedes with warmth and charity, but the granddaughter will have nothing to do with this strange, distant relative. So Mercedes must spend her meager funds in a boarding house, where she falls prey to delinquents who cheat her out of her money. Having located an amateur variety hall where she can make her debut, she convinces the old grandmother to lie to her family, sneak out of the house, and attend. Mercedes is a complete failure on stage, and the old lady, seeing Mercedes's only hope as returning to her husband, writes to him. The husband replies that he would welcome his wife back, so when Mercedes appears at her relatives' house a few weeks after her disastrous "debut," the grandmother encourages her to consider returning to her husband and children, showing her the husband's letter. Mercedes accepts the dignified escape from her predicament that the grandmother has organized for her and returns to the village.

A number of minor themes suggested in this novelette are developed more fully in the novels: (1) The feminist motif has several dimensions: (a) Mercedes, as a woman subordinated to her family's wishes, was forced to marry an unsuitable man and curtail her desire for a career. She is sacrificed to family decorum. (b) The old grandmother is a prisoner in her granddaughter's house, because she has no money of her own. She has never worked, having lived from cradle to grave dependent on the support of others: her parents, her husband, her children, and now her grandchildren. Thus she arrives at old age at the mercy of relatives, who are only waiting for her death and who do not even give her pocket money for an occasional charity or whim. (2) The charity theme is introduced through the grandmother figure. She represents an earlier, prewar generation in Spain, before Spaniards became mean-spirited and greedy in the deprivation of the post–Civil War period. She is generous and kindly with the slightly demented Mercedes. Lolita, the granddaughter, an example of postwar mentality, will not even consider aiding Mercedes. Although the narrative style of "The Vocation" lacks the vitality characteristic of Laforet's best writing, authorial sensitivity in portraying the odd and touching relationship between Mercedes and the grandmother carries the novelette and partially compensates for the less successful choice of narrative technique.

"El último veraneo" (The Last Summer) reiterates the charity theme, which was only a leitmotif in "The Vocation" but is central to "The Last Summer." The characters are contrasted one with another in their concepts of charity. The crystallizing situation is the doctor's appraisal that Doña Pepita, mother of three sons, will not live out the year. The two younger sons, who still live at home, decide to scrape together the money necessary to give their mother the summer vacation in San Sebastián that she has always wanted and which the sacrifices of raising a family in post–Civil War Spain have denied her. The oldest son is married to Lolita, a selfish girl, who does not want her husband to contribute to the project. She is pregnant and wants their savings to go toward their own summer vacation, which she feels necessary in her condition.

"The Last Summer" is one of Laforet's best-constructed short novels. With the dying mother as a focal point, each character's aspirations, as well as other family members' perceptions of him, are revealed. Luis, the youngest son, is the only one to be given an education; all the family members contribute to his schooling. Luis does not enjoy studying and often skips classes to engage in various activities with his friends. Several times he has acted as an extra in films being shot on location and has thereby earned 800 *pesetas* with which he had planned to buy a bicycle; however, he willingly contributes the money to the fund for his mother's summer vacation.

Lucas, the middle son, is the most morally oriented and the most concerned with organizing the trip. His family scorns the girl he has chosen to marry, because she is a seamstress and her family socially inferior, but Lucas recognizes her moral qualities. She, in contrast to Lolita, gives her 1,000-*peseta* savings to Lucas for the mother's trip, whereas Lolita, who has much more and who is already part of the family, refuses to give anything. Lucas finally convinces the oldest son, Roberto, to take 2,000 *pesetas* out of their savings without telling Lolita so that the fund may be completed. Roberto prefers to take out a loan, at exorbitant interest, which he will have to repay by allowing himself no luxuries for two years, in order to conceal the contribution from his wife.

The novelette masterfully captures the aspirations and pretensions of Spain's postwar middle class. Doña Pepita represents all the frustrated values of this class which, before the conflict displayed its affluence by educating its children, having servants, and summering in San Sebastián. But, whereas Doña Pepita's generation has accepted its lot, Lolita is typical of the penurious, self-centered younger generation, struggling to achieve economic status. Luis has a poetic bent, but he hides his poetry from the rest of his family, knowing they would be disappointed at his lack of interest in other studies leading to a career. He often feels oppressed by the closeness and lack of privacy in the family ambience and considers escape: "The idea of his family obsesses him" (N, p. 718). These motifs contribute to the richness of the central story.

In "The Last Summer" Laforet uses the technique of interior/exterior ambiences to substantiate characterization—a technique central to the short stories. For example, both Lucas and Luis walk through the city streets when they are upset; this allows them the distance and freedom from family that they require to explore their consciences and their problems as individuals. They are members of a family, which limits their movements, but they are also individuals, who must ultimately seek their own place in life. Luis is disturbed when he receives word that he has failed an entire year of school:

The high school was in a working-class district. Women passed by hurriedly with their baskets on their arms. They had little time left to get the meal on the table. Jingling street cars passed, as well as carts and cars. There was a little cart stopped at an intersection. A donkey was pulling it. A man, on foot, was leading the animal, and on top of the load—some piled up sacks—, was a dirty child and a dog. They seemed to be in their glory, and Luis envied them.

The little cart set off. And Luis, fascinated and feeling open to wandering, decided to follow it out of pure whim. He had decided to think a bit before going home. (N, pp. 717–18)

Lucas takes to the street late at night after having an argument with Roberto and Lolita over their contribution to the mother's summer vacation. He has had a miserable day; in the emotion of learning of his mother's terminal illness, he forgot a date with his fiancée and she reacted angrily. The street is the appropriate place for him to reflect upon the events of the day:

He was on a wide street with trees, that permitted one to see through them to a high, dazzling sky. A fresh odor, coming miraculously from the distant mountains, turned into pure asphalt... A great silence, a blessed silence filled the world. Lucas would have liked to have had a glass of wine to lift his spirits, but all the bars in the neighborhood were closed and the windows of the houses dark. Only the stars shone. Being there was like being alone on earth. That night was like a night in the country during vacation.

—My God!—sighed Lucas aloud. —My God!

In the great silence, God seemed to listen.

Lucas began to feel less wretched. He walked slowly through the long empty street, looking in fascination at the jeweled sky. (*N*, pp. 709–10)

All the characters except Lolita undergo transformation in face of Doña Pepita's impending death. The normal, trivial preoccupations and pretensions of their class fall away: the family accepts, or at least overlooks, Luis's failure at school and Lucas's fiancée is welcomed into the family. Only Lolita continues to see the world from the vantage point of her petit bourgeois values. When she sees Doña Pepita with a new coat made especially for the trip, she secretly thinks what a waste of money it is for a dying woman to spend so much on an item she will use only one summer. "The Last Summer" seems ultimately to raise the same moral issue which lies at the center of *The New Woman*: the limits and extension of personal rights to fulfill individual needs for growth when juxtaposed with the obligations of the individual to the social construct. Once again the family serves as a compact microcosm in which to examine this fundamental human problem. The conclusion of this novelette is the same as that of *The New Woman*, that the individual can achieve personal aims by prior submersion in the social world. Otherness in these works is a prerequisite to individuation and maturation.

Although the Spanish Civil War is alluded to in many of Laforet's works, "El viaje divertido" (The Pleasure Trip) and "Los emplazados" (The Condemned) are the only pieces to incorporate the hostilities as a significant theme or milieu. These novelettes, which directly project the horrors of the conflict either in memory or reality, may be spin-offs of *The New Woman*, which was in preparation at the time of their writing. It is quite likely that they are alternative modes of handling the Paulina-type character—a young woman whose life hinges on Civil War experiences. In "The Pleasure Trip," Elisa, like Paulina, is apparently ill-suited to marriage, household management, and child care. Elisa worries continually that she is not a good wife and mother, and her doctor-husband, Luis, does much to undermine her self-confidence by constantly pointing out how easy her life is. Elisa and her sister-in-law Rosa must go to Madrid for a wedding in the family; exigencies of work prevent their husbands from accompanying them. It is the first time that either woman has traveled on her own. Rosa, of much stronger personality than Elisa, assures the latter that they will have a grand time in the city—a veritable pleasure trip. Her prediction results in a great irony, because the experience becomes a nightmare for both of them and leads to significant changes in their lives.

On the train, Elisa faints after seeing her cousin Javier, also traveling to Madrid for the family wedding. Elisa believes she recognizes in him the man who took her parents from their home one day during the Civil War. The parents were later found shot on a roadside and the family home completely ransacked (it was believed in the village that Elisa's father had a fortune hidden somewhere on his property). Although the circumstantial evidence of Javier's guilt was never substantiated (he bought part of the property from Elisa's husband), his behavior at the wedding, including several uncouth and violent acts, casts further suspicion upon him, at least in Elisa's mind.

Elisa conceals her suspicions until she sees Rosa becoming friendly with Javier during their stay in Madrid. She confides in her kindly mother-in-law, who, in turn, tells Elisa of Rosa's youthful infatuation with Javier. The family had rejected Javier as a suitor for Rosa, because he is a coarse, lazy, unadmirable person, and forced her to marry another man. The mother-in-law relays Javier's possible criminality to Rosa, who becomes so agitated that she cannot appear at the wedding celebration. During the party, Javier, in a drunken fit, terrorizes everyone by shooting into a mirror. Rosa attempts to clear Javier's reputation with Elisa, but alleges she has overcome her romantic feelings for him. Somewhat relieved and reassured after these intense encounters, the two women return to the village.

In the meantime, the two husbands back home in the village play chess together. Rosa's husband, José, is jealous and suspicious of his wife's freedom in the city. Rumors have filtered back to the town that their wives behaved in an indecorous fashion at the wedding party, that they even danced the can-can. When the women return home, José refuses to meet them at the train station, but Luis goes to meet Elisa. He inexplicably lies about their little girl's health, saying that she is sick (seemingly to cause Elisa to feel guilty at having been away). Elisa rushes home to find her daughter in perfect health. The tender repartee between husband and wife over this incident reveals a genuine affection each for the other that had perhaps always existed in the marriage, but that neither had previously recognized.

The homecoming motif in "The Pleasure Trip" is much more powerful than in the novel *The New Woman*. The return to husband and family is based on psychological need rather than on moral duty. Laforet finely draws the psychology of a young woman who has married and had children very early, before having experienced the world. Although only twenty at the time of the trip, Elisa has been married for three years and has two children. Her infantile dependence on her husband before the trip becomes a mature appreciation of him afterward. He too changes his attitude toward his wife. The home-versus-world dialectic that provides the basic tension of the novelette is subtly introduced in the opening paragraphs. Elisa and Luis are lying in bed asleep in the early morning hours. Elisa gradually becomes cognizant of the world as she awakens:

The world seemed submerged. Fog was coming in from the forests, and that damp canopy beneath the mountain peaks, serving as a roof to the little village in the valley gave a feeling, from the interiors of the houses, that day would never come. The sounds of water running, dripping, enriching everything could be heard.

Elisa was hearing those sounds of water from the depth of sleep. The room in which the couple slept was large. . . . A large triparite wardrobe, a huge bed and two cribs seemed to swim in it. Dark curtains were drawn in front of the closed balcony. . . . Outside, that house which lodged them was large and good. (*N*, p. 963)

In the rest of the novelette, Elisa enters the world, encounters evil, and returns home renewed—wiser and more aware. Evil is introduced via the unscrupulous, mystery-shrouded male figure as it was in *Nothing*; Javier has much in common with Román, but lacks his artistic talent. "The Pleasure Trip" also shares with *Nothing* the use of several unresolved enigmas resulting from incidents that occurred during the Civil War. Elisa's early childhood impressions of the strife, her parents' murder, and her subsequent encounters with the possible murderer, Javier, are inserted in movielike flashbacks that build the terror of the confrontation with Javier on the train and at the wedding. The murder-mystery part of the story is not solved, but the tension and foreboding it creates is dissolved, as it is in "Los emplazados" (The Condemned), with felicitous matrimony.

"The Condemned" is Carmen Laforet's only fictional foray into the realm of the fantastic. She borrows the beginning of the fairy tale "Sleeping Beauty," in which an old lady not invited to the christening curses those present and predicts the child will die in a fixed number of years. In Laforet's short novel, a neighbor not invited to baby Teresa's baptism claims to see the devil holding up four fingers, supposedly signaling that four people at the gathering are marked to die in twenty years. The story thus begins realistically enough—the old lady's "vision" can be explained as her retaliation for not having been invited to the baptism. But then the narrative focus shifts to an omniscient view of the baptismal feast, and the devil incarnate appears with no subjective distortion intervening. The devil recognizes the condemned people: the baby Teresa; Nicanor, a heretical relative; Nicolasillo, his nephew; Paquito Gómez Gaya, a small child; and a young soldier who lives in the same apartment building as Teresa's parents. The devil is surprised that there are five rather than four and suspects a reversal of his plans.

In the next section of the novelette, twenty years have elapsed, and it is September of 1936. The Civil War has been in progress for some three months, and the Nationalists have just captured the town where Teresa is a schoolteacher. The young soldier who was present at her baptism is now a commander in the Nationalist army; Paquito Gómez Gaya is an officer under him, and Nicolasillo is a soldier in Paquito's command. Don Nicanor has been killed by Republicans. Paquito finds lodging for his men in the school buildings with Teresa's aid. None of the condemned recognizes any of the others as guests at Teresa's baptism.

Paquito falls in love with Teresa, who is flirting with him in order to prolong their tour of the school buildings; she is afraid to return to her house, where a Communist mine leader is hiding. That night, by happy coincidence, Paquito goes to Teresa's house to ask for the key to the school library (a pretext to see her) and arrives just at the moment the mine leader is preparing to rape Teresa. Paquito mistakes Teresa's willingness to accompany him back to the school for acquiescence to his own growing desire for her. She angrily rebuffs his advances, but nonetheless chooses to remain in the library with the gentle Paquito, rather than return to the house and the crude mine leader.

Nicolasillo spots the mine leader escaping from Teresa's house during the night; he is shot, and Teresa is accused of treason for harboring an enemy. Paquito covers for her in court, convincing the commander that Teresa was with him, that they are engaged to marry, and that she had nothing to do with either the Republicans or the mine leader. The other piece of incriminating evidence in the case is the discovery of a photograph of Lenin in Teresa's house. Laforet seems to be satirizing the political naiveté that characterized the various factions in the Spanish Civil War: the photograph ultimately turns out to be of Teresa's father.

Teresa is exonerated, and while she and Paquito are celebrating over lunch, a blast rocks the entire town. The town hall has been blown up. Had Paquito not convinced the commander of Teresa's innocence, he, Teresa, the commander, and Nicolasillo—all four earmarked by the devil twenty years earlier—would have been present at a War Council in the city hall to try Teresa's case at that very moment. Thus, as in "Sleeping Beauty," the prophecy is almost fulfilled, but the "princess" is rescued by the young man who falls in love with her. Three of the condemned later recognize that they were guests at Teresa's baptism, recalling the neighbor's vision of the devil and her prediction that four people would die in twenty years. Paquito comments on this incident: " 'It seems to me, Teresa, that this is just a traditional folktale that your family attached to you!....' "(N, p. 959). But the omniscient narrator refuses to allow this realistic explanation of the baptismal tale to stand as the final word: "And so the story of the condemned remained a story that the condemned themselves did not even recognize" (N, p. 959).

Rather than a story about devils or romantic love during the horrors of war, "The Condemned" is concerned with the truth of storytelling itself versus the truth of life. A story is not a story until it is recognized as such by an agent outside the boundaries of the tale; each life is a potential story that generally remains unrecog-

128   CARMEN LAFORET

nized by its protagonists. Laforet heightens the self-consciously fictional nature of her own tale by setting it within the framework of a traditional folktale recognizable to nearly everyone. Although "The Condemned" is not one of Laforet's best pieces, by combining contemporary political history with traditional folk material she has produced an interesting experiment in fictional modes of portraying the division between life and literature. In "The Pleasure Trip" and "The Condemned" (both written in the early 1950s), Laforet has achieved the necessary temporal distance from the Civil War to use its thematic power in her literary treatments of evil. In *Nothing* the war remains submerged almost entirely, and it is only of peripheral concern in *The Island and the Devils*. It is as though in writing these two novelettes she wished to test the possibilities of combining personal and political history. Many of the characters of her longer works (Juan, Gloria, Román, Matilde, Paulina, Eulogio, Eugenio) could have been the center of a story about their psychology or circumstances determined by the war. But Laforet seems to have discarded this kind of direct use of war settings and political theme in the longer works, where she prefers to suggest rather than state the political motifs.

The writer's dilemma when using a highly charged political backdrop to develop human emotions of universal concern is to keep the political issues from dominating the human ones. Laforet's solution in the longer works—to filter the political contexts through memory (she does this even in "The Pleasure Trip")—is one that becomes common to many Spanish writers of the post–Civil War period. Seemingly only a few foreign writers (e.g., Hemingway, *For Whom the Bell Tolls*, or André Malraux, *Man's Hope*) were able to use the Spanish Civil War as an effective setting for a novel of universal and lasting significance. The political issues in that war (fascism, international communism, republicanism, and anarchism, among others) were too well defined and too intense to allow for depolitization even in literature.

Like *The New Woman*, "El piano" (The Piano) explores the psychology of a young married woman. Rosa possesses many traits of other Laforet heroines: she is terribly thin and not especially pretty, but has a certain elegance and physical charm. Rosa is a nonconformist who smokes and exhibits a great penchant for freedom. She asserted her independence at an early age by choosing not to live with a wealthy, domineering aunt when she was orphaned. The financial security of the aunt's home and legacy were not enough reward to exchange for her freedom. Due to Rosa's stubbornness, the aunt leaves Rosa nothing in her will except a grand piano; the aunt had always enjoyed hearing Rosa play. At the time she inherits the instrument, Rosa is married to Rafael, a would-be novelist. Their life is extremely modest, but they arrange a room especially for the piano in their tiny apartment. Their lives begin to center on the music room, in which they enjoy concerts given by a musically talented friend.

When both Rafael and their child fall seriously ill, they must sell the piano to pay the debts incurred for medicines. On the day the piano is to be removed from the apartment, Rosa, instead of going to work, devotes the day to shopping, spending some of the piano sale money on luxuries (e.g., books). She feels free, wandering about the city, in contrast to her usual confinement in the office. But her carefree spirit dissolves when she returns home to the empty music room. She bursts into tears before Rafael, who is using the room to work on his novel. The tender reassurance they give each other reinforces the main message of the novelette: that the mainstay of life is human compassion and understanding predicated on truth and freedom. The piano, the material object, symbolizes freedom gained; even its sale represents freedom from debt. If Rosa had complied with her aunt's wishes, and given up her adolescent freedom, she would have inherited a fortune, but her relationship with Rafael would doubtless have suffered. The only time they ever argued was over how they would spend their inheritance from the aunt (during her deathbed illness they believed they would be heirs). Rafael has a tendency to prefer grandeur and showy living, which Rosa tempers with her realism and simplicity.

"The Piano" and many other pieces written during Laforet's "Christian" period tend to trite themes; their interest lies in finely wrought characters and in their narrative approaches. "The Piano" constitutes a narrative experiment in some ways. Much of the story is told by several earthy street types who discuss the life of Rafael and Rosa, that atypical, "artistic" family, from a distance. The old woman candy-seller, fond of Rosa, defends her unconventional behavior to other neighbors. Luisa, Rosa's maid, takes the narrative reins at one point to relate a sort of intercalated folktale that has nothing to do with the principal story line. Luisa, like Vicenta in

The Island and the Devils, is a stalwart peasant woman who has unlimited loyalty to the family she serves. She stays with Rafael and Rosa even though they cannot pay her for months at a time. Luisa's tale, like Vicenta's section in *The Island and the Devils*, is a narrative tangent centering on the function of storytelling per se.

"La niña" (The Little Girl), according to the author herself, is based on real-life figures: a *beata* (an extremely religious woman who devotes much time to church-related activities)[3] and a little girl. Even though she does not mention who these people are, Carmen Laforet herself looms large behind the *beata* figure, Carolina. The writer noted after rereading the novelette years later:

Upon encountering the *beata* figure now in reading "The Little Girl," I realize that in all or nearly all the works of Carmen Laforet [she speaks of herself in the third person here] written between the years '52 and '55, one finds either the word *beata* or some personage of feminine religiosity, treated with special tenderness for such a discredited literary figure. The author believes that perhaps this phenomenon occurs as a reaction to the repugnance that this word inspired in her in childhood. The word *beata* suggested the most coarse human caricatures to her. Perhaps for that reason, upon finding herself in a spiritual state, unprotected by the walls of intellectual restraint that had been natural to her, she underwent a change of values even in the meanings of [some] words, and the word *beata* surprised her by recovering its meaning of woman who has happiness, who has reached beatitude.[4]

Despite this insistence on the *beata's* importance in "The Little Girl," the central figure is the child herself, Olivia. Olivia is like the hub of a wheel with a world of self-centered adults revolving around her. She only partially perceives their motives as they relate to her and her situation. Olivia is an orphan whose dying mother charged Carolina, a lay sister at the hospital, with taking her daughter to an orphanage. The mother, a widow, had been living a bohemian life with a painter. The latter, a selfish type, sees the mother's death as relieving him of a burden; the boy child they had together is packed off to his paternal grandmother, and Olivia is to enter an orphanage; he will be free again.

Carolina's story is unfolded as a secondary plot in the novelette, secondary because Carolina relates her history to her stepdaughter Asunción as they sit by Olivia's bedside waiting for her to fall asleep.

A sunción's mother was Carolina's sister, and gossip has it that Carolina had always wanted the father for herself and had even hastened her sister's death in order to marry her brother-in-law. Carolina's stepchildren believe this fabrication, despising Carolina. The truth that Asunción learns at Olivia's bedside is that Carolina had a religious vocation and would have preferred to remain single, but the disastrous state into which her sister's family fell after the sister's death suggested to Carolina that she could do the greatest work of charity and love by marrying her brother-in-law in order to take care of her nieces and nephews. (The story seems to be borrowed from Unamuno's *La tía Tula*.)

Olivia overhears this conversation and then falls asleep. The next day Asunción finds another house for Olivia; there is no room for her at Carolina's, even for the few days she must wait to enter the orphanage. Olivia is to be hidden in the rooms of the housekeeper at the palatial home of Asunción's boyfriend. The charm of the novelette derives primarily from the child's perspective, from which the walk to the new house and brief stay there are narrated. Olivia's perception is always blurred by her shadowy understanding of the adult world; she is incapable of putting into perspective the things she overhears or of drawing any conclusions about the data she receives. Her child's attention is always focused on the present:

Olivia began to like seeing new things. . . . Now that she had resigned herself to leaving Carolina's house, she no longer thought about her, and with each step she took in the streets on that splendid spring day, she felt more and more adventuresome and curious. (*N*, p. 879)

An incident that occurs during Olivia's brief stay with Teresa, the housekeeper, reveals her child's imagination and accurately portrays child psychology in its perennial ability to manipulate adults in order to escape punishment. Teresa leaves Olivia alone in her room for several hours, and Olivia, growing bored, uses a chair as a horse, falls, and hits her head against the closet. At this moment Teresa returns and finds Olivia frightened. Teresa, a superstitious woman, is convinced that the former cook is haunting her room. She is certain that Olivia has heard or seen the apparition. Her suspicion is confirmed when Olivia's imagination and desire to keep Teresa from inspecting the damage in the closet invent the presence of a little old lady in the room. Olivia has transformed the image of the Virgin over the bed into her grandmother, with whom she remem-

Virgin over the bed into her grandmother, with whom she remembers attending Mass several years earlier; there was a similar image in the church. Teresa triumphantly announces to her employers, who have been scoffing at her visions, that she has a witness to the ghostly presence. When she produces Olivia and encourages her to repeat her experience, the little girl has already forgotten the lies she spun to cover up her mischievousness. When asked what she saw in Teresa's room, she blurts out that there was a large commode under the bed. Olivia is saved from Teresa's anger by the fortuitous arrival of her grandmother. Having learned of her daughter-in-law's death, the grandmother has come to take Olivia to live with her.

As the happily reunited grandmother and granddaughter travel through the countryside in their third-class train car, there is one final insight into the child-mind of Olivia. The little girl sees a vagabond with a knapsack tied to a stick and remembers Alberto, the painter, in whose house she lived for several years: "That name of Alberto, for a second, was in the little girl's throat, in her violently beating little heart. But it had only been an instant, that in which the train passed the nameless vagabond... Then, Olivia forgot him forever" (N, p. 896). One is tempted to assume that "The Little Girl" is either a spin-off of The New Woman or a short exercise related to the longer novel. The beata Carolina naturally invites comparison with Paulina. Whereas the longer novel is a psychological study of the beata personality and her struggle of conscience, the novelette's beata has a truly religious vocation, yet suffers no conflict. Carolina is a flat character, a foil to the little girl. The achievement of "The Little Girl" is to suggest in some detail the essentials of so many adults' lives through the eyes of a six-year-old child. At least seven adults (Carolina; Luis, her brother-in-law/husband; Asunción; Alberto; the painter; María, Olivia's mother; and Teresa, the housekeeper) are portrayed in their aspirations and frustrations from the child's vantage point. Olivia serves as a catalyst and crystallizing agent in the lives of all these people. She is the real center of attention as vehicle of the narrative focus. The beata and the attendant themes of charity and self-sacrifice are peripheral to the most significant feature of the novelette—the viewpoint itself.

"El noviazgo" (The Engagement) is likely Laforet's best piece of short fiction; of all her work, it is perhaps second only to Nothing in terms of literary accomplishment. The novelette is often anthologized and has been published in a separate, annotated school edition.[5] "The Engagement" seems somewhat out of place in the series of novelettes composed during the early 1950s while Laforet was working out her own spiritual crisis and writing *The New Woman*. Because it seems thematically unrelated to the other novelettes, I discuss it last. It was, however, apparently written at roughly the same time as the others. The themes of self-sacrifice and charity prevalent in the short stories written between 1951 and 1955 and in all the other short novels (1951–1952) are absent here. In fact, "The Engagement" could be interpreted as militantly feminist in its conclusion: a woman rejects a seemingly desirable marriage in a hostile display of latent bitterness and self-assertion.

Alicia, a fifty-year-old spinster, has been secretly in love with her boss, De Arco, during the thirty years she has worked for him. In order to shield herself from her mother's prying, Alicia has completely suppressed her emotional life, slowly becoming a severe and embittered old maid. Adding to her burden is the attitude toward work that her social background has instilled in her. Under normal circumstances a woman of Alicia's social class would consider work tabu, but Alicia has had to help support the family since her father's premature death. Her physical appearance underscores the paucity of her emotional life and her ineffectual pretensions to aristocracy. She is small, with petite, pretty features. She keeps her bleached-blond hair in tight curls and wears frilly, fussy, slightly out-of-date clothes.

Her only escape from a reality that does not attain the level of her expectations is to build a fantasy world in which her family tree rivals that of De Arco, who has inherited the title of marquis. In her imagination, Alicia transforms her father's modest two years as secretary to a consul in England into an ambassadorship and converts a distant cousin whose sister is married to a count into nobility in the immediate family. She is extremely proud of her lofty-sounding last names, Quiñones y Álvarez de la Torre, and uses them at inappropriate moments. De Arco, now a widower, proposes marriage to Alicia, imagining how pleasant it would be to spend his old age cared for by this woman who has clearly loved him for so long. But Alicia's reaction, beautifully captured in several dialogues with her mother and with De Arco, is negative and recalcitrant. Alicia discovers that she has come to hate De Arco for the humiliation he has always made her feel; her overriding sentiment at being asked for her hand in marriage is to humiliate in return. Alicia demands a large, formal wedding with many guests, which De Arco, old and unwilling to appear ridiculous, refuses. Alicia is unbending in her demands for a wedding "befitting her social class," and, in a tragicomic luncheon scene witnessed by Alicia's emotionally over-wrought mother, rigid, old-fashioned Alicia and a gout-stricken De Arco call off the engagement.

Laforet's portrayal of Alicia in all the details of her psychological development is magnificent. Despite the difficulty of maintaining verisimilitude in drawing a character of this type and keeping the portrait from becoming an overdrawn caricature, Laforet never loses control of the delicate strings that move Alicia's seemingly irrational and inexplicable behavior. Her self-sentencing to a life of eternal work, penury, and spinsterhood is incomprehensible to her mother and to De Arco, but the reader sympathizes with her reaction be-cause he is privy to Alicia's interior life during thirty years of un-requited love and self-denial.

The dream/reality theme, which does not occupy a central place in Laforet's fiction after *Nothing, The Island and the Devils*, and the early short stories, makes a powerful comeback in "The En-gagement." Alicia's dreams and illusions about her social station are paralleled by De Arco's fantasies of a blissful second marriage to Alicia. He discusses his project in a fanciful conversation with the portrait of his dead wife:

—Well, I've made a choice... What do you think?
—I think you're getting senile, poor dear. What in the world do you think that humorless creature is going to do in this house?
—Well, my dear, she'll take care of me... And, besides that, she has never lived; it will be like marrying a little girl, without the dangers of marrying a child... It will be a new experience to travel with her, teach her how to dress, to make her enjoy the comforts she has never known, and, finally, to discover her most intimate side, which is so locked up; to hear her confess the affection she has felt for me all these years, even back in the days when you, on your rare visits to my office, told me that she was the ideal secretary for me, because, without being ugly, she was the living incarnation of "unattractiveness." (*N*, p. 760)

The impact of Alicia's refusal to marry De Arco is all the greater for the carefully constructed mutual illusions that are destroyed in one monumental scene at the restaurant. A finely orchestrated exchange of illusions and reality takes place: when Alicia's dream of attaining De Arco's social status becomes a possible reality, her world dissolves; when De Arco faces the reality of an embittered, hostile woman rather than a grateful, acquiescent future wife, his illusion vanishes.

As in many of Laforet's best works, space is an important adjunct to creating the characters. Alicia's office is small, but filled with light from the patio window; she blends perfectly with this tiny, well-kept room. To reach De Arco's office, she must cross a large, overwhelming library, representative of the social gap between them and the emotional sacrifice each meeting with her boss means for the secretary:

She self-assuredly crossed an immense library, where she became a very small little thing dressed in pale green among the thousands of volumes accumulated first out of intellectual curiosity and then out of the inertia of three generations. Years before, when Alicia crossed that room, she felt invariably timid and stifled by the beating of her heart; it seemed to her that she would never reach the other side, the door of De Arco's office. Now the immense glassed-in shelves, the statues of white marble, the oak tables on which no one ever placed a book to read, all that cold sumptuousness of a museum had become something of an insignificant routine. (*N*, p. 739)

Alicia's house is small and cramped; she has no private space there, because she and her mother share one bedroom, having rented the other to a boarder. These small quarters reflect the narrowness of spirit to which Alicia has been reduced. The point is casually made in the car en route to the engagement luncheon that Alicia has never spent time in the country. Her final explosion of haughty demands is as large as the space she has always been denied. The psychological and spatial crescendo toward the culminating refusal scene is resolved in Alicia's satisfying words:

—Well, I have the pleasure, Mr. De Arco, of rejecting your proposal of marriage... I have the pride to refuse to be your wife... Do you understand? I refuse to be your wife.

Alicia was theatrical, magnificent. She forgot everything and felt happy. It was a very shortlived happiness, but splendid. De Arco, from his stature, seemed shorter than she. It was as though she were slapping him. (*N*, p. 785)

There are only three characters in the novelette, and each is a masterpiece. Carolyn Galerstein has pointed out that Alicia has a prototype in Angustias (even to the detail of the boss's having taken refuge in the secretary's home during the Civil War).[6] But Angustias is seen through Andrea's eyes and thus unsympathetically; in the case of the novelette, the reader is in complete sympathy with Alicia, because her story is told entirely from her point of view. The mother (one of the rare mothers in Laforet's fiction) is a fine portrayal of the middle-class Spanish lady whose world centers on her house and her gossip. Alicia, true to her old-fashioned ideas about male/female relationships, insists that her mother accompany her and De Arco (as a chaperone) during their engagement luncheon: "Alicia appeared accompanied by a large and very excited lady under a black hat... In reality one could say that Alicia was accompanied by a great black mass furnished with a fur, a hat, a purse, gloves, tight shoes, and inside all that paraphernalia, a lady throbbed and blushed" (*N*, p. 776). Doña Ana's reactions to Alicia's strange behavior throughout the luncheon define Alicia's mania and simultaneously characterize her own shallow mentality. For its felicitous blend of psychological insight and descriptive detail, "An Engagement" will remain one of Laforet's strongest and most successful pieces of fiction.

CHAPTER 6

The Achievement

M OST critics who have considered Laforet's work as a whole
find in retrospect great unevenness in the quality of the individual pieces, not so much in the writing itself (which most agree
is nearly always lively and felicitous) but in the view of life projected.[1] Laforet has been especially taken to task for stories and
novelettes of the "Christian" period such as "A Marriage," "The
Christmas Gift," and "The Last Summer" for their seemingly cheerful and unrealistic acceptance of self-sacrifice. They have been called
novelas rosas (escape literature)[2] and criticized as not rising "above
the level of fiction in women's magazines."[3] My purpose in writing
this volume has not been to vindicate Laforet's work in the face of
these judgments (any writer has some works that are better than
others). Rather, I have attempted to show how each piece of Laforet's writing fits into her complete fictive canon and to understand
the most effective elements of each novel or story. While granting
that some of Carmen Laforet's writing has not contributed as much
as has the best of her production (especially *Nothing*, parts of the
other novels, and several of the stories and novelettes), I wish in
this summary to reemphasize the strengths rather than the weak-
nesses.

A concluding evaluation and overview might effectively stress the
position Laforet's fiction commands in the panorama of Spanish
post–Civil War fiction. To this point I have deliberately minimized
references to Laforet's contemporaries in order to build a solid view
of her creation as an individual writer. Such an approach is perhaps
more valid in the case of Laforet than with, say, Miguel Delibes,
Camilo José Cela, or Ana María Matute, whose artistic vision has
been shaped by direct experience of the Spanish Civil War. Laforet's
personal isolation during that event and her post-facto arrival on the
mainland are as significant to her view of the world as the war itself
was to her contemporaries. Laforet is further distinguished from

other members of her novelistic generation by her intense religious experience.

But, though her formative years are different, at age eighteen Laforet did enter the world of her contemporaries and, at age twenty-two, joined in the move to rebuild Spanish literary production, which had been demolished by the war. As the author of the second important novel to be published after the Civil War, she was instrumental in exploring new narrative paths to deal most effectively with the novelistic material at hand, namely, the Civil War and the sociopolitical situation of the postwar years. The methods of treating this material had to be oblique for two reasons: (1) censorship was rigid, and (2) artistic taste requires a balanced emphasis between topical matter (e.g., politics or a particular society) and universal human concerns (growing up, love, death, etc.).

Spanish fiction of the post–Civil War period can be divided into roughly four chronological stages, using the decades as loose boundaries. (It should be understood that this is a simplification signaling general trends.) The 1940s did not produce a distinctive, unified literary picture; they were a time of exploration and experimentation. *Tremendismo*, seemingly unmotivated violence and an emphasis on ugliness and horror (said to have been invented in 1942 by Cela in *La familia de Pascual Duarte*), was a feature many works had in common. Laforet's *Nothing* has been called a psychological variant of *tremendismo*. By the 1950s the examples of the Italian neo-realistic cinema and this country's socially realistic novelists of the 1930s (Steinbeck, Dos Passos, Hemingway, and Faulkner) provided Spanish novelists the models they needed for treatment of their own social reality. The Spanish novel from the late 1940s to the early 1960s tends to focus on some aspect of Spain's social ills (poverty, country versus city, land ownership, industrialization, worker conditions, the Church) in a fairly straightforward, "realistic" style. The artistic merit of many of these novels is dubious, and their topicality severely limits their interest for later generations and foreign readers. In many ways Laforet's *The New Woman* participates in this mood of social criticism.

The publication of Luis Martín Santos's *Tiempo de silencio* in 1962 marks a beginning of shifts in techniques and themes in the Spanish novel. Martín Santos added a mythic dimension to his still relatively plain, uninnovative narrative techniques (I refer to overall structural tactics; his language is immensely complex and ironic).

The course set by Martín Santos (who, unfortunately, was killed in an automobile accident before completing any more novels) was elaborated and enriched by others with innovations in narrative voice and structural experimentation that by the early 1970s could rival the French novelists, who had been experimenting with narration since the early 1940s. The Spanish narrative of the 1960s gives the impression that the writers are struggling to become comfortable with the new techniques (e.g., multiple viewpoint, second-person narrative voice, achronology, structure anchored in images rather than action). Salient examples of these experiments include Delibes's *Cinco horas con Mario* and *Parábola del náufrago*, Cela's *San Camilo 1936*, Juan Goytisolo's *Señas de identidad*, and Juan Benet's *Una meditación*. The 1970s have seen a maturation in these writers as they have learned to accommodate the innovations to their personal concerns and styles. The current renaissance in the Spanish novel promises still further high-quality work.

While in the comprehensive picture of the Spanish novel of the post–Civil War period, Laforet's production has not evolved comparably with that of her contemporaries, she sowed seeds that have been cultivated by others. Surely the single most important contribution Laforet has made to the Spanish novel in general is the indirect treatment of the Spanish Civil War found in nearly all her novels and stories. The conflict is a reality to all Spaniards, either as a lived experience or to later generations as something retold by relatives and friends. Laforet manages to convey in fiction just that aspect: the experience of the war *after* the war, when it can only be a memory or a retold story. She accomplishes this through momentary flashbacks, overheard conversations, intercalated tales, etc. Her satisfying method of achieving artistic distance from painful personal and political events by removing the narration to a second or third voice becomes one of the hallmarks of Spanish fiction of the 1960s. Delibes's Menchu sustains a one-sided dialogue with her dead husband, recounting their entire marriage (*Cinco horas con Mario*); Juan Goytisolo's *Señas de identidad* is narrated to an unidentified listener, and Carmen Martín Gaite's *Retahílas* is a dialogued memoir, to mention only a few examples of comparable distancing.

Laforet, too, is a precursor of and a model for employing the family paradigm to reflect society at large. One encounters fairly obvious imitations of the use of the family in *Nothing* (cf. Ana María

Matute's *Los Abel*), as well as many interesting variations on the
theme. Incest and adultery enter into Delibes's fictive families (*Las
ratas* and *Cinco horas con Mario*), while Carmen Martín Gaite
studies the effect of parental separation on children in *Fragmentos
de interior*, and Ana María Moix's *Julia* examines an aberrant
mother-daughter relationship. Many novelists have found the concept of family generations appropriate to their view of history and
society. Not only does the family paradigm provide a compact microcosm for dealing with a particular society, it lends itself readily
to the universalizing dimensions of archetype and myth. And it is
primarily through these avenues that the Spanish novel became
able to move beyond the narrow limits of social introspection of its
1950s stage.

Carmen Laforet's primary plot dynamic in the longer novels is
a quest for identity, not unlike that of the great myths analyzed by
the psychologists Carl Jung and Otto Rank. The use of mythic over-
tones as a universalizing agent for specific social and political material is found in many European and American novelists who could
easily have served as models for the Spanish novel of the 1960s and
1970s (James Joyce, William Faulkner, the Latin American "Boom"),
but one should not overlook the fact that the earliest Spanish novels
of the post–Civil War period (e.g., *The Family of Pascual Duarte*
and *Nothing*) had already demonstrated the possibilities thereof.

In this summary I wish once again to emphasize Carmen Laforet's
importance for the female novelists who followed her. The debt
these authors owe Laforet is twofold: (1) Her Nadal award opened
the way for greater acceptance of fiction by women. Never again
could the male critics, prize-givers, and novelists be unreceptive
to work written by women. (2) She invented numerous literary
methods by which women could write about subjects important to
their lives (e.g., relations to brothers and parents, marriage, motherhood, spinsterhood, the Church, confinement, and discrimina-
tion) in ways that would not seem partisan or propagandistic—in
short, of limited interest. Laforet drew many of her characters from
the ranks of stock Spanish female types—the *beata*, the spinster,
the frustrated career woman, the kindly, self-effacing grandmother—but she always manages to avoid caricature. She imbues
each woman with her psychological rationale and complex set of
circumstances. Some of her secondary characters are absolutely
unique (e.g., Vicenta and Frufru). The heroines of her long novels

are nonconformists but believable because their confrontations with
social limitations to their personal freedom are dialectical,[4] producing gradual growth and adjustment. Even the least convincing
"Pollyannas" (Isabel of "The Christmas Gift" or Rosa of "The Piano")
are given some psychological ambiguity. We see them at a trium-
phant moment, but they have fallen to depressive lows before and
well may again.

Criticism to the effect that Laforet's male characters are not well
developed psychologically[5] may be valid for the earlier work, but
in *Sunstroke* she convincingly portrays Spanish male psychology.
In the earlier novels, men are primarily negative role models or
potential partners to be encountered and rejected. Also of especial
importance to Spanish women is the role of the Catholic Church
in their lives; it is a major obstacle—through its moral code on
childbirth, divorce, and women's roles—to women in Spain looking
for alternatives to marriage and motherhood. Laforet crossed the
traditional tabus against dealing with such topics frankly and openly,
particularly in *The New Woman*. She also took on another contro-
versial and touchy subject—homosexuality—in *Sunstroke*. In both
of these works the oblique approach is the key to her success.
Finally, it should be pointed out that in several respects Carmen
Laforet's fiction is very much a part of the long and important history
of Spanish narrative, which began in 1554 with the publication of
Lazarillo de Tormes, a series of picaresque episodes welded together by the unique vision of their adolescent protagonist, who
gradually and painfully learns that life is a struggle and that one
must lose a few illusions on the road to survival. Laforet was one
of the first of a number of post–Civil War novelists to rediscover
the novelistic possibilities of adolescent lives in a loosely structured,
episodic format.

One of Laforet's central concerns, the conflict between human
dreams and aspirations and the limitations placed on them by reality,
has its roots in *Don Quixote*, the first fullfledged Spanish novel,
written early in the seventeenth century. Laforet even uses Cervantes's fundamental approach to this life dichotomy by embedding
opposing views in pairs of characters.[6] With her compatriot Galdós,
she has in common an interest in character types and physical surroundings, but she forgoes Galdós's love of objective, descriptive
detail for highly personal, "artistic" distortions of reality. As explained above, one of her most outstanding achievements is the

fusion of fantasy and reality as a theme with an artistically elaborated style to underscore that theme. There have been a number of translations into many different languages of Carmen Laforet's works, especially of *Nothing*. The latter is translated into English, French, German, Dutch, Swedish, Polish, Czech, and perhaps others (neither Laforet nor her publishers have a complete list of all translations, since copyright considerations are not always honored). Several film versions of *Nothing* have been attempted, without great success. Laforet herself is quite interested in the film medium and has projected a collaboration on a film version of the "Rosamunda" story.

In 1977 Carmen Laforet was named an Honorary Fellow in the Society for Spanish and Spanish American Studies for her outstanding contribution to Spanish letters, a well-deserved recognition. Her literary production to date assures her place in the ranks of the Spanish novel since 1940, and that secure place may be enhanced by future work. Each of her four long novels is in some sense an interpretation of a significant aspect of contemporary Spanish history seen through the eyes of an individual caught up and enmeshed in it. Andrea discovers Barcelona immediately after the end of the war; Marta views from a distance the progress of the conflict and its conclusion; Paulina, having been shaped by prewar Spain and experiences of the hostilities, changes and grows along with the postwar Spanish society of the 1950s. Martín lives in a provincial, isolated, post–Civil War Spain that is juxtaposed to a warring Europe. If Laforet remains true to her artistic canon of the past—interpreting an historical period through individual lives—we can look forward, hopefully, to her artistically insightful views of Spain in the 1960s and 1970s and perhaps later decades.

Notes and References

Chapter One

1. From an autobiographical sketch especially prepared (in Spanish, translation is mine) by Carmen Laforet for the author of this volume in June 1976.
2. Carmen Laforet, "Encuentros con Galdós," *El Urogallo* 1 (1970): 67.
3. She shares with the *novecentistas* (Gabriel Miró, Ramón Pérez de Ayala, and Ramón Gómez de la Serna), her immediate Spanish predecessors in the Spanish novel, an emphasis on imagery and the use of elliptical modes of narration. But her overall achievement has little in common with that of the *novecentistas*, who concentrated on linguistic and aesthetic concerns, rather than on the narrative itself, which preoccupies Laforet.
4. Carmen Laforet, "Introducción" to *Mis páginas mejores* (Madrid: Editorial Gredos, 1956), p. 10.
5. See note 1.
6. Laforet, "Introducción" to *Mis páginas mejores*, pp. 10–11.
7. See note 1.
8. *Books Abroad* 30 (1956): 394.
9. 9:418 (1945): 13.
10. "Carta a Carmen Laforet," *Ínsula* 3:25 (1948): 1.
11. Carmen Laforet, *Carmen Laforet* (a collection of articles), ed. H. E. Leigh (Sussex, Eng.: Stuart Spencer Publications, 1978).
12. See note 1.

Chapter Two

1. "Introducción," *Mis páginas mejores*, p. 8.
2. "Unas líneas de la autora," in *Novelas*, I (Barcelona: Editorial Planeta, 1957), p. 11.
3. "Balance de verano," *Informaciones*, September 21, 1953, p. 8.
4. "Diario de Carmen Laforet," *ABC*, April 14, 1972, p. 52.
5. Graciela Illanes Adaro, *La novelística de Carmen Laforet* (Madrid: Editorial Gredos, 1971), p. 18.

6. "Introducción," *Mis páginas mejores*, p. 8.

7. "Al sur de Gran Canaria," *Información Comercial Española*, April 1952, p. 483.

8. Carmen Laforet, *Novelas*, I. All references to Laforet's novels and stories are taken from this edition, except for *Sunstroke*, which is not included in the volume.

9. "La casa," *Informaciones*, October 24, 1953, p. 10.

10. "Diario de Carmen Laforet," *ABC*, December 15, 1971, p. 61.

11. Ibid., February 9, 1972, p. 43.

12. "Horas de Tánger," *ABC*, n.d. (probably 1971), n.p.

13. "Diario de Carmen Laforet," *ABC*, March 25, 1972, p. 53.

14. Ibid.

15. Louis Rubin, *The Teller in the Tale* (Seattle: University of Washington Press, 1975), p. 120.

16. "El reloj interno," *Destino*, August 4, 1951, n.p.

17. "La imagen del pasado," *Informaciones*, March 25, 1954, p. 1.

18. "Diario de Carmen Laforet," *ABC*, December 3, 1971, p. 47.

19. Margaret E. W. Jones, "Dialectical Movement as Feminist Technique in the Works of Carmen Laforet" in *Studies in Honor of Gerald E. Wade* (Madrid: José Porrúa Turanzas, 1979), pp. 110–111.

20. "Diario de Carmen Laforet," *ABC*, April 12, 1972, p. 53.

21. "Poesía cálida," *Destino*, November 24, 1951, p. 7.

22. "El mapa íntimo," *Destino*, February 17, 1951, p. 11.

23. "Difícil valoración," *Destino*, March 17, 1951, p. 7.

24. "Una opinión de mujer sobre la feminidad," *Destino*, July 14, 1951, n.p.

Chapter Three

1. Carmen Laforet, *Nada*, ed. E. R. Mulvihill (Oxford, Eng.: Oxford University Press, 1960).

2. M. Fernández Almagro, " 'Nada' por Carmen Laforet," *ABC*, August 12, 1945, p. 31.

3. "*Nada* by.Carmen Laforet: A Venture in Mechanistic Dynamics," *Hispania* 35 (1952): 210.

4. Richard Chase, *The American Novel and Its Tradition* (Garden City, N.Y.: Doubleday, 1957), pp. 12–13, quoted in David William Foster, " 'Nada' de Carmen Laforet," *Revista Hispánica Moderna* 32 (1966): 45.

5. (Barcelona: Editorial Planeta, 1973), pp. 177–201.

6. Elizabeth Ordóñez, "*Nada*: Initiation into Bourgeois Patriarchy," in *The Analysis of Hispanic Texts: Current Trends in Methodology*, eds. Lisa E. Davis and Isabel C. Tarán (Jamaica, N.Y.: Bilingual Press, 1976), pp. 62–63.

7. Michael D. Thomas, "Symbolic Portals in Laforet's *Nada*," *Anales de la Novela de Posguerra* 3 (1978): 57–74.

8. Sara E. Schyfter, "The Male Mystique in Carmen Laforet's *Nada*," to be published in *Novelistas femeninas de la postguerra española*, ed. Janet W. Díaz (Madrid: José Porrúa Torranzas). Another feminist treatment of *Nada* is found in Celita Lamar Morris, "Carmen Laforet's *Nada* as an Expression of Woman's Self-Determination," *Letras Femeninas* 1 (1975): 40–47. Professor Morris bases her study on sociological material about the actual situation of women in Spain.

9. After the completion of this manuscript there appeared Robert Spires's essay "La experiencia afirmadora de *Nada*," in *La novela española de posguerra* (Madrid: Cupsa Editorial, 1978), pp. 51–73. Professor Spires analyzes the dynamics of the dual narrative perspective pointed out by El Saffar, in terms of the interaction between Andrea's active being and her contemplative self. He demonstrates that the distance between these two perspectives is reduced and finally fused as the novel progresses. Professor Spires employs the useful concept of the implied reader to discuss the impact of the lyrical passages and the play of light and dark in the novel. While Professor Spires and I use quite different terminology, I believe my own analysis in section IV ("The Role of Art in *Nothing*") points in the same direction as his, namely, that the ultimate effect of *Nothing* is to produce an attitude of positive creation through the dialectic narrative technique.

10. Ruth El Saffar, "Structural and Thematic Tactics of Suppression in Carmen Laforet's *Nada*," *Symposium* 28 (1974): 119.

Chapter Four

1. "La segunda novela de Carmen Laforet," *Revista de Literatura* 1 (1952): 236–37.

2. "En el Puerto de la Luz," *Destino*, April 14, 1951, p. 10, and "Noche canaria," *Destino*, April 21, 1951, p. 10.

3. Carmen Laforet, *La insolación* (Barcelona: Editorial Planeta, 1963), p. 322. All references to this novel are from the same edition.

4. Ordóñez, p. 71.

5. Erich Neumann, *The Great Mother* (Princeton, N.J.: Princeton University Press, 1955), pp. 279–80.

6. Sven Armens, *Archetypes of the Family in Literature* (Seattle: University of Washington Press, 1966), pp. 45–46.

7. Carl G. Jung et al., *Man and His Symbols* (New York: Doubleday & Co., 1964), p. 125.

8. Armens, p. 20.

9. Ibid., pp. 34–35.

Chapter Five

1. Introductory note by the author to "Cuentos," in *Novelas,* I, 263.
2. Introductory note by the author to "La llamada," in *Novelas,* I, 639.
3. I do not attempt to translate this word in my discussion here: none of the English equivalents—beatified woman, devout woman, bigot, prude—captures the idea as Laforet means it. *Beata* for her includes each of these qualities.
4. Carmen Laforet, "Prólogo" to *La niña y otros relatos* (Madrid: Editorial Magisterio Español, 1970), pp. 9–10.
5. Carmen Laforet, *Un noviazgo,* ed. Carolyn Galerstein (New York: The Odyssey Press, 1973).
6. Carolyn Galerstein, "Carmen Laforet and the Spanish Spinster," *Revista de Estudios Hispánicos* 11 (1977): 311.

Chapter Six

1. The studies that treat Laforet's work as a whole include Cyrus C. DeCoster, "Carmen Laforet: A Tentative Evaluation," *Hispania* 40 (1957): 187–91; María del Pilar Palomo, "Carmen Laforet y su mundo novelesco," *Monteagudo* 22 (1958): 7–13; J. Horrent, "L'Oeuvre Romanesque de Carmen Laforet," *Revue des Langues Vivants* 25 (1959): 179–87; Pierre Ullman, "The Moral Structure of Carmen Laforet's Novels," *The Vision Obscured: Perceptions of Some Twentieth Century Catholic Novelists* (New York: Fordham University Press, 1970), pp. 201–19; Margaret E. W. Jones, "Dialectical Movement," and Graciela Illanes Adaro, *La novelística de Carmen Laforet.*
2. Gonzalo Sobejano, "Carmen Laforet," in *Novela española de nuestro tiempo* (Madrid: Editorial Prensa Española, 1970), pp. 122–23.
3. DeCoster, p. 190.
4. Jones, "Dialectical Movement."
5. DeCoster, p. 191.
6. Jones, "Dialectical Movement."

Selected Bibliography

PRIMARY SOURCES

"El infierno." *Insula* 1 (1944): 2.
Nada. Barcelona: Editorial Destino, 1945.
La isla y los demonios. Barcelona: Editorial Destino, 1952.
La muerta. Barcelona: Editorial Destino, 1952.
"Recién casados." *Ínsula* 100–101 (1952): 20.
"El secreto de la gata." *Bazar* 60 (1952): 3–4.
La llamada. Barcelona: Editorial Destino, 1954.
La mujer nueva. Barcelona: Editorial Destino, 1955.
Novelas, I. [Includes *Nada*, "La muerta," "El veraneo," "La fotografía," "En la edad del pato," "Última noche," "Rosamunda," "Al colegio," "El regreso," "Un matrimonio," "El aguinaldo," *La isla y los demonios*, *La llamada*, *El último verano*, *Un noviazgo*, *El piano*, *La niña*, *Los emplazados*, *El viaje divertido*, *La mujer nueva*.] Barcelona: Editorial Planeta, 1957.
La insolación. Barcelona: Editorial Planeta, 1963.
Paralelo 35. Barcelona: Editorial Planeta, 1967.
La niña y otros relatos. Madrid: Editorial Magisterio Español, 1970.

SECONDARY SOURCES

The following list is highly selective, including only substantive critical articles on Laforet's work, and excluding any book reviews or articles in literary manuals or histories.

1. Book
ILLANES ADARO, GRACIELA. *La novelística de Carmen Laforet*. Madrid: Editorial Gredos, 1971. The only book-length overview of Laforet's fiction in Spanish. Of the thirteen chapters, four cover the full-length novels, interspersed with chapters on recurrent themes and motifs in Laforet's work; two chapters deal with the short fiction. Parts are

insightful (especially the chapter on *La insolación*), but on the whole, lacks critical depth.

2. *Articles*

DECOSTER, CYRUS C. "Carmen Laforet: A Tentative Evaluation." *Hispania* 40 (1957): 187–91. A survey of Laforet's work prior to *La insolación*. Finds that Laforet has not lived up to the achievement of *Nada* in subsequent work.

EL SAFFAR, RUTH. "Structural and Thematic Tactics of Suppression in Carmen Laforet's *Nada*." *Symposium* 28 (1974): 119–29. An excellent article pointing to the ultimate pessimism of *Nada* as revealed through the dual narrative perspective.

EOFF, SHERMAN. "*Nada* by Carmen Laforet: A Venture in Mechanistic Dynamics." *Hispania* 35 (1952): 207–11. An attempt to equate the structure of *Nada* with a mechanistic world-view in which people are objects moved by forces beyond themselves.

FEAL DEIBE, CARLOS. "*Nada* de Carmen Laforet: La iniciación de una adolescente," in *The Analysis of Hispanic Texts: Current Trends in Methodology*, ed. Mary Ann Beck et al. Jamaica, N.Y.: Bilingual Press, 1976, pp. 221–41. A psychoanalytic study exploring the male/female dimension in Andrea's relations with all the characters. Demonstrates that Andrea's views and personal situation undergo change.

FOSTER, DAVID WILLIAM. "'Nada' de Carmen Laforet." *Revista Hispánica Moderna* 32 (1966): 43–55. Isolates and discusses the characteristics that *Nada* has in common with modern versions of the Romance genre or Gothic novel.

GALERSTEIN, CAROLYN L. "Carmen Laforet and the Spanish Spinster." *Revista de Estudios Hispánicos* 11 (1977): 303–15. Analyzes and compares the spinster figure in the novels and stories where she occurs. Concentrates on Alicia of "Un noviazgo" (An Engagement) and Angustias of *Nada*.

GLENN, KATHLEEN M. "Animal Imagery in *Nada*." *Revista de Estudios Hispanicos* 11 (1977): 381–94. Indicates how Laforet employs animal imagery to enhance her concise character portraits. Interesting comparison with Cela's use of animals in *La familia de Pascual Duarte*.

HORRENT, J. "L'Oeuvre Romanesque de Carmen Laforet." *Revue des Langues Vivants* 35 (1959): 179–87. An overview in French of the long novels (except *La insolación*) with a few references to the short fiction. Generally positive, but has reservations about *La mujer nueva*.

JONES, MARGARET E. W. "Dialectical Movement as Feminist Technique in the Works of Carmen Laforet" in *Studies in Honor of Gerald E. Wade*. Madrid: José Porrúa Turanzas, 1979, pp. 109–20. Useful comparison of the structuring method based on character pairs in both the long and short novels. Concludes that the dialectical movement involved in these pairs creates the underlying novelistic tension.

LAMAR MORRIS, CELITA. "Carmen Laforet's *Nada* as an Expression of Woman's Self-Determination." *Letras Femeninas* 1 (1975): 40–47. Using as background material the social status of women in Spain in 1942 and 1943, the article discusses Andrea as a woman asserting her independence.

NEWBERRY, WILMA. "The Solstitial Holidays in Carmen Laforet's *Nada*: Christmas and Midsummer." *Romance Notes* 17 (1976): 76–81. Points up the incongruity produced by juxtaposing the bizarre events of the house on Aribau Street with holiday festivities.

ORDÓÑEZ, ELIZABETH. "*Nada*: Initiation into Bourgeois Patriarchy" in *The Analysis of Hispanic Texts: Current Trends in Methodology*, eds. Lisa E. Davis and Isabel C. Tarán. Jamaica, N.Y.: Bilingual Press, 1976, pp. 61–78. Thesis that the patriarchal bourgeois family in *Nada* is a reflection of post–Civil War Spanish social structure is well argued. Demonstrates that Andrea's choices are manipulated toward her final entry into the patriarchal bourgeoisie.

PILAR PALOMO, MARÍA DEL. "Carmen Laforet y su mundo novelesco." *Monteagudo* 22 (1958): 7–13. Written upon the publication of the first volume of complete works (*Novelas*), this study finds the protagonist's search for life to be the common motivating element of the first three long novels.

SCHYFTER, SARA E. "The Male Mystique in Carmen Laforet's *Nada*" (to be published), in *Novelistas femeninas de la postguerra española*, ed. Janet W. Díaz. Madrid: José Porrúa Turanzas. A perceptive study of the negative influence of the male in the social development of the female. Focuses on Román's relationships with the women characters.

SPIRES, ROBERT C. "La experiencia afirmadora de *Nada*," in *La novela española de posguerra*. Madrid: Cupsa Editorial, 1978, pp. 51–73. Taking into account the implied reader, this excellent study analyzes the dynamics of the dual narrative perspective of the novel (active being and contemplative stance).

THOMAS, MICHAEL D. "Symbolic Portals in Laforet's *Nada*." *Anales de la Novela de Posguerra* 3 (1978): 57–74. Fine article that pinpoints four key narrative moments in which the protagonist recognizes her maturation process while standing before or upon passing through a doorway. Concludes that *Nada* is "an affirmation of life and not a denial of it."

ULLMAN, PIERRE L. "The Moral Structure of Carmen Laforet's Novels," in *The Vision Obscured: Perceptions of Some Twentieth Century Catholic Novelists*. New York: Fordham University Press, 1970, pp. 201–19. Finds Laforet's novels to be essentially Catholic, even *Nada*, which was written prior to Laforet's "conversion" to Catholicism, because they convey a moral point of view.

VILLEGAS, JUAN. " 'Nada' de Carmen Laforet o la infantilización de la aventura legendaria," in *La estructura mítica del héroe*. Barcelona: Editorial Planeta, 1973, pp. 177–201. An article of fundamental importance, showing *Nada*'s affinity to other twentieth-century European novels in which the protagonist's actions follow essentially the pattern of those of a mythic hero, who progresses through a series of significant adventures and stages toward maturity.

Index

Adler, Alfred, 77
Alberti, Rafael, 31
Archetypes, 92–98, 140
Art, 16, 19, 23, 41, 42, 53, 54–66, 68, 69, 70–71, 72, 74, 75–76, 86, 88, 90–91, 92, 113, 141–42
Autobiography, 14, 41–43, 54, 106, 117, 143n1
Ayala, Francisco, 25
Azorín (José Martínez Ruiz), 25–26

Benet, Juan, 35; *Una meditación* (A Meditation), 139
Berceo, Gonzalo de, 113
Böll de Faber, Cecilia, 13
Booth Wayne, 42
Burell, Consuelo, 20

Cain and Abel, 15, 49
Canary Islands: 16, 23, 68–69, 73; See also Carmen Laforet
Catholic Church, 77–78, 82–84, 141
Catholicism; 45, 50, 67, 149; See also Carmen Laforet
Cela, Camilo José, 16, 35, 137; *familia de Pascual Duarte, La* (The Family of Pascual Duarte), 44, 138, 140, 148; *San Camilo, 1936*, 139
Cerezales, Manuel, 25, 26
Cervantes, Miguel de: *Don Quixote de la Mancha*, 17, 141
Cézanne, Paul, 72
Charity, 29, 100, 104, 107, 109, 118, 120–21, 131, 132, 133

Delibes, Miguel, 35, 137; *Cinco horas con Mario* (Five Hours with Mario),

36, 139, 140; *camino, El* (The Road), 76; *guerras de nuestros antepasados, Las* (The Wars of Our Ancestors), 36; *Parábola del náufrago* (Parable of a Shipwrecked Man), 36, 139; *ratas, Las* (The Rats), 140
Dos Passos, John, 138
Dreams, 40, 57, 59, 63, 74, 134

Existentialism, 47, 51
Expressionism, 58–59

Family, 14, 34, 52, 60, 68, 70, 92–98, 122, 139–140
Fastenrath Prize, 25
Father figure, 85, 87, 95–98
Faulkner, William, 35, 45–46, 69, 72, 138, 140
Feminism, 43–46, 89, 93, 100, 120, 133, 140
Film versions of works, 142
Freud, Sigmund, 77, 96
Friendship, 18, 21–23

Ginsburg, Allen, 40; *California Trip*, 40
Gómez de la Serna, Ramón, 143n3
Goya, Francisco, 60
Goytisolo, Juan, 16; *Señas de identidad* (Marks of Identity), 139
Goytisolo, Luis, 35

Hemingway, Ernest: 14, 26, 138; *For Whom the Bell Tolls*, 128

Impressionism, 58–59

Jiménez, Juan Ramón, 25, 26, 47
Joyce, James, 17, 35, 140; *Portrait of the Artist as a Young Man*, 54

151

152   *Index*

Jung, Carl, 94, 96, 140
Jungian psychology, 95

Laforet, Carmen, ancestors, 14–16; as a
university student, 21–24; childhood,
15–20; children, 26, 118; conversion,
28–29; father, 16–17, 18–19; ideas on
writing, 33–35; in Canary Islands,
19–20, 76; in Poland, 30–31; in Rome,
31–32; in United States, 30; journalistic writing, 30, 33, 36, 39; marriage,
26, 28, 31; mother, 16–18; stepmother, 19

WORKS: BOOKS
Insolación, La (Sunstroke), 13, 29, 39,
44, 67, 84–92, 94, 97, 141
Isla y los demonios, La (The Island and
the Devils), 13, 27, 39, 41, 67,
68–76, 77, 84, 92, 93, 94, 96, 99,
101, 103, 128, 130, 134
Llamada, La (The Vocation), 29, 99,
118–19; "llamada, La," 118, 119–21;
"noviazgo, Un" (An Engagement),
113, 118, 132–36; "piano, El" (The
Piano), 114, 118, 128–30; "último
verano, El" (The Last Summer),
118, 121–23, 137
Muerta, La (The Dead Woman), 27,
37, 99; "Al colegio" (Off to School),
99, 100, 106–107; "En la edad del
pato" (At the Awkward Age), 99,
107; "fotografía, La" (The Photograph), 99, 100, 105–106, 111;
"muerta, La," 99, 100, 107–109,
111; "regreso, El" (The Return), 99,
103–104, 111; "Rosamunda," 99,
100, 101–102, 109, 119; "Ultima
noche" (The Last Night), 99,
100–101; "veraneo, El" (The Summer Vacation), 102–103, 111
Mujer nueva, La (The New Woman),
13, 28–29, 39, 46, 67, 76–84, 92, 94,
96–97, 99, 106, 107, 123, 124, 132,
133, 138, 141
Nada (Nothing), 13, 16, 21, 24–26, 28,
30, 31, 35, 39, 41, 47–66, 67, 68–69,
74, 76, 85, 87, 92, 95, 101, 104, 108,
112, 125, 128, 133, 134, 137, 138,
139, 140, 142

Niña y otros relatos, La (The Little
Girl and Other Narratives), 100
Novelas, I: "aguinaldo, El" (The
Christmas Gift), 100, 109–10, 111–12,
137; "emplazados, Los" (The Con-
demned), 118, 126–28; "matri-
monio, Un" (A Marriage), 99, 109,
111, 114, 137; "niña, La" (The Little
Girl), 118, 130–132; "viaje diver-
tido, El" (The Pleasure Trip), 118,
123–26; see also *isla y los demonios,
La; llamada, La; muerta, La; Nada;
niña y otros relatos, La Paralelo 35*
(Parallel 35), 14, 30
Tres pasos fuera del tiempo (Three
Steps Out of Time), 29

WORKS: JOURNALISTIC WRITING
"Diario de Carmen Laforet", 27–28,
106
"Puntos de vista de una mujer," 27–28,
106

WORKS: UNCOLLECTED STORIES:
"alivio, El" (The Unburdening), 100,
115–17
"infierno, El" (The Inferno), 100,
112–13
"Recién casados" (The Newlyweds),
100, 113–15
"secreto de la gata, El" (The Cat's Secret), 100, 117–18

Lafuente, Pablo, 31
Latin American "Boom", 140
Lazarillo de Tormes, 17, 141

Machismo, 85, 89–90, 94
Malraux, André: *Man's Hope,* 128
Martín Gaite, Carmen: 46; *Fragmentos
de interior,* 140; *Retahílas,* 139
Martín-Santos, Luis, 138
Matute, Ana María, 16, 35, 46, 137; *Los
Abel,* 139–40
Medio, Dolores, 46
Memory, 40–41, 42, 54, 59, 63, 66,
108–109, 128, 139
Menorca Prize, 28
Miró, Gabriel, 143n3; *Niño y Grande,*
113; *obispo leproso, El,* 113

Moix, Ana María: 46; *Julia*, 140
Mother figure, 19, 70, 73, 77, 85, 89–95, 97, 98, 106
Mysticism, 79–80
Myth, 51–52, 95, 97, 140

Nadal Prize, 13, 25, 140
Neumann, Erich: *Great Mother, The*, 94; *Origins and History of Consciousness*, 98
Novecentistas, 143n3

Painting, 15, 16, 39, 49, 60, 71, 90–91, 92
Pardo Bazán, Emilia, 13
Pérez de Ayala, Ramón, 143n3; *A.M.D.G.*, 113
Pérez Galdós, Benito, 17, 35, 141, 143n2
Picasso, Pablo, 22, 60, 61, 71, 91–92
Proust, Marcel, 14, 17–18, 35, 41–42; *Within a Budding Grove*, 59

Quiroga, Elena, 46

Rank, Otto, 140

Salinas, Pedro, 35
San Juan de la Cruz, 33, 79, 111
Santa Teresa, 33–34, 79
Sender, Ramón, 25, 30
Society for Spanish and Spanish American Studies, 142
Space, 36–41, 73–74, 108, 111–12, 122, 135
Steinbeck, John, 138
Surrealism, 59
Spanish Civil War, 16, 20, 21, 24, 47, 48, 49, 66, 68, 69, 70, 78, 88, 96, 120, 123–24, 126, 127, 128, 136, 137, 138, 139

Tangiers, 39–40
Tremendismo, 47, 138

Unamuno, Miguel de: *tía Tula, La*, 131

World War II, 22, 23, 24, 27, 61, 86, 88, 91, 92, 142

Van Gogh, Vincent, 71
Vázquez Zamora, Rafael, 35, 45

Zayas de Sotomayor, María, 13